THE STATE AND ECONOMIC DEVELOPMENT

T0347343

THE STATE AND ECONOMIC DEVELOPMENT
Lessons from the Far East

Edited by

ROBERT FITZGERALD

FRANK CASS · LONDON

First published in 1995 in Great Britain by
2 Park Square, Milton Park,
Abingdon, Oxon, OX14 4RN

and in the United States of America by
FRANK CASS
270 Madison Ave, New York NY 10016

Transferred to Digital Printing 2005

British Library Cataloguing in Publication Data

State and Economic Development:Lessons
from the Far East. – (Studies in Far
Eastern Business, ISSN 1351-0363)
  I. Fitzgerald, Robert   II. Series
  338.95

    ISBN 0 7146 4638 5 (hardback)
    ISBN 0 7146 4159 6 (paperback)

Library of Congress Cataloging-in-Publication Data

The State and economic development : lessons from the Far East /
  edited by Robert Fitzgerald.
      p.   cm. — (Studies in Far Eastern business)
    "This group of studies first appeared in a special issue of Far
  Eastern business, vol. 1, no. 3 (Spring 1995)" — T.p. verso.
    ISBN 0-7146-4638-5. — ISBN 0-7146-4159-6 (pbk).
    1. Industrial policy—East Asia.   2. Industrial policy—Asia,
  Southeastern.   3. East Asia—Economic policy.   4. Asia,
  Southeastern—Economic policy.   I. Fitzgerald, Robert.   II. Series.
  HD3616.E18S73   1995
  338.95—dc20   94-44155
                                                              CIP

This group of studies first appeared in a Special Issue of
Far Eastern Business, Vol.1, No.3 (Spring 1995),
[The State and Economic Development: Lessons from the Far East].

Typeset by Vitaset, Paddock Wood, Kent

Contents

Abstracts

The State as Economic Engine: Lessons from the Japanese Experience, *by Charles J. McMillan.*

The historical relationship between business and government in Japan contrasts with the methods and ideological battles to be found in the West, where understanding has continuously lagged behind Japanese practice. Government ministries in Japan have been important to the objectives of technology acquisition, resource allocation, and export-orientated growth. They have involved themselves in the microeconomic details of industrial structure, and, following a rigorous investigation of the issues, they have achieved a coordinated and relentless pursuit of specific economic aims. Yet overall state expenditure as a percentage of GDP has remained low, and vigorous competition has always been preferred to centralised blue-prints and the selection of single national champions. The cooperative, dualistic relationship between business and government in Japan has correctly assessed and adjusted to the realities of global competition in the ruthless search for sales and productivity. Western perplexity at the workings of the Japanese industrial system has given rise to notions of national uniqueness, but the industrialising countries of East Asia are looking not to the West but to the Japanese mix of market and state.

Economic Theory and Industrial Policy in East Asia, *by Tan Kock Wah and Jomo K.S.*

Economic liberalisation has been advocated as universally valid for developed and developing countries alike, and, as a result, the role of the state has been disparaged in favour of unrestricted markets and free trade. The neo-classical proposition is by no means fully justified from a theoretical point of view, and there exist powerful, countervailing arguments why government intervention and market coordination, especially during a nation's initial stage of industrialisation, can achieve improved resource allocation and greater competitive advantage. By helping to explain the very creation of industrial capacity, as well as the enhancement of long-term growth rates, institutional economics can provide clearer insights into the complementary roles of state and market. These theories are, moreover, supported by empirical evidence from East Asia, where government has been a contributory but not dominant factor in the achievement of economic success.

Economic Development and the State: Lessons for Singapore, *by Tan Kong Yam.*

Analysis and case studies have indicated that intervention by the Singapore government in fostering economic development has not always been successful. In particular, past intervention in the labour market like the high wage policy of the early 1980s has proved to be an unmitigated disaster. However, interventions that lead to the direct creation of national competitive advantage, like the information–telecommunications infrastructure, R & D subsidy and manpower development, have proved to be more successful. A strong, non-corrupt and market-oriented public sector appears to be crucial to ensure that interventions are market facilitating, correcting and enhancing rather than distorting.

The State and Business Relations in Taiwan, *by Hsin-Huang Michael Hsiao.*

Taiwan's government has been characterised by a strong, authoritarian system, and it has proved willing to intervene in the nation's economic development. There exists, however, an important division between large-scale, domestic-orientated industries and those which have supplied export markets, and the less dynamic sector has often received the government's favour. But the increasing success of Taiwan's export manufacturers, their very contribution to the process of industrialisation, has gradually strengthened their influence within official policy making, and their progress has been assisted by more recent democratisation.

Changing Business–Government Relations in Korea, *by Ku-Hyun Jung.*

Business–government relations in Korea were transformed during the developmental period between 1960 and 1990 under an authoritarian government. The relationship could be characterised as a close and vertical one where the government took a firm control of the business sector through the allocation of financial resources and entry permits for new business. Cultural characteristics such as close family and school ties and the Confucian tradition of respecting civil servants helped to strengthen this relationship. However, there have been signs that the traditional 'Korea, Inc.' model has outlived its usefulness. As the economy matured and became more open to the world economy, the tight control of the economy by bureaucrats has proved less effective and in many cases it has weakened the efficiency of the economy. The democratisation of the polity has also changed the traditional vertical relationship among the power elite, bureaucrats and business. Now the government has become just one of the many stakeholders that business has to interact with in a more pluralistic and decentralised society.

The Evolving Role of Government in China's Transitional Economy, *by John Wong and Kang Chen*

This paper recounts the changing economic role of Chinese government, both at the central and local levels, in the reform process. The previously all-encompassing role of the central government has been greatly reduced, mandatory plans abolished, prices decontrolled, and administrative controls decentralised. Decentralisation has reoriented the interest of local governments towards reform and system innovation, fostered a climate for reform initiatives and spontaneous reform at local level, and induced competition among different localities that has again provided incentives for local governments to change, to adapt to changes, and to innovate. Decentralisation, however, has also led to dilemmas and problems, and created instability and uncertainty in China's macro-economic conditions and central–local relations.

The Private Sector as the Engine of Philippine Growth: Can Heaven Wait?, *by Manuel F. Montes*

Taking a sceptical view of the 'Asian miracles' proposition that government failure is the main culprit behind development failure, this article reviews the Philippine development experience. The Philippine configuration consists of a weak state carrying out industrial promotion and a large private sector whose dynamics depend heavily on state-managed privileges. In the final section, the article proposes an alternative to the rent-seeking model, in which rents defined as returns contingent on political position and rivalry over political position determine private investment behaviour. In such a society, there is limited internal basis for structural change and growth is accidental to external developments.

Preface

The relationship between industrialisation, national competitive advantage and the role of the state concerns an issue of recognised vintage. The mercantilist systems of the eighteenth century, gravitating around Europe, became the subject of contemporary debate and political controversy and, finally, firm lessons were deduced from the experience of minimalist government and modern economic growth in Victorian Britain. But, in recent decades, historians have compared the circumstances and achievements of the first industrial nation with the growth of various European powers. It would be wrong to reduce the complexity and subtleties of each case to the comfort of a simplistic framework, but at least the sufficiency of efficient price mechanisms and the neo-classical paradigm alone were challenged.[1]

The economic role of the state was too ideological and too difficult a controversy to be easily resolved within the leading industrialised nations of the post-war world, but several trends eventually brought a move away from governmental activism. The internationalisation of the economy undermined policies of protectionism and, while political economy had once focused on social justice, ownership, and class control of the state machinery, competitiveness emerged as a primary national objective. The domestic policies of Reagan and Thatcher, worldwide privatisation, and the collapse of the planned, Communist economies all seemed to augur an era of state withdrawal from the marketplace, just as the Bretton Woods institutions ensured that many debtor countries underwent a prescription of reduced government deficits and price adjustments. Yet at the very point at which a great intellectual debate and an even greater ideological battle appeared to be won, the rise of the East Asian nations reintroduced the old uncertainties and complexities.

The neo-classical perspective is based on the notion that there is only one form of capitalism, thereby ignoring the influence of organisations, institutional relationships, stages of economic development, and the context set by resources, demand factors, culture, and historical legacy. The Far Eastern countries not only posed the view that there are more forms of capitalism than the Anglo-American variety, however dominant it may have appeared in the 1980s, but they also raised the notion that they possessed a competitively superior form of capitalism. Their economies differed from the USA and Britain, and even from Western Europe, in many respects, but one identifiable feature was the contended existence of a developmental state.[2] It was possible to interpret their national economic success as the result of low government expenditure and a determination to enforce price mechanisms,[3] or, where the assistance of export-orientated industrialisation was recognised, the state was said to be acting as would any market actor. In contrast, others argued for government supremacy or, more convincingly, that there was a symbiotic relationship between the state and the private sector.

The East Asian economies were market-driven, but government influenced decision-making, output and export priorities in a way that helped fulfil nationally-agreed objectives. Moreover, most notably in the obtainment of industrialisation and in the establishment of key industries, the state could correct failures in the market mechanism. While neo-classical economics offered lessons on how to operate a capitalist system, the textbooks were less explicit about how to put a capitalist system together. Through a mixture of market-led growth and state direction, the advantages of competition, diversity, and control were combined with stability, the protection of vital, nascent industries, and the encouragement of long-term perspectives towards training, investment, and research.

Not all economies were capable of industrialisation, high growth rates, and impressive export records, and not every government proved able to accelerate development. Each national situation has to be judged separately, and the gains to be found in economic liberalisation and integration into the world economy are equally variable. The relationship between business and the state also evolves as the economy matures, and industrial, social and political priorities alter alongside new competitive demands.

In this volume, the contribution made by the Japanese state to its country's development is explored, and the rationale behind state-led growth, East Asian imitation of the Japanese model, and Western perplexity at the phenomenon are all covered. In addition, the advantages of state-business interaction are grounded in economic theory, and the case of Singapore stands as an example of this symbiosis. But the evidence of Korea and Taiwan demonstrates both the costs as well as the benefits of government intervention, especially as pressures associated with alterations in the nature of politics and the structure of industry continue to rise. The momentous events of rapid growth in mainland China, linked to changes in state policy and power, are investigated. If the state alone is unable to secure national economic success, it does seemingly have the power to prevent its occurrence, and, in this volume, the Philippines reveals how a poor record, far from being ideologically tainted, is not automatically linked to planned economies.

In asking why East Asia has industrialised, when so many parts of the world have proved incapable, declarations solely on behalf of the state are not an adequate answer. But, in Japan and the Four Tigers, government has acted as a substitute for private enterprise, whenever market mechanisms appeared the less effective means of achieving a nationally strategic objective. Business groups, bank-industry relationships, and the ties between buyers and suppliers often act in a similar way, yet to dismiss the positive contribution made by state direction and activism is, as the contributors to this volume demonstrate, to misread the so-called East Asian miracle.

Robert Fitzgerald

NOTES

1. See A. Gershenkron, *Backwardness in Historical Perspective* (Cambridge, MA, 1966); A. Milward and S.B. Saul, *The Development of the Economies of Continental Europe, 1850–1914* (London, 1977); C. Trebilcock, *The Industrialisation of the Continental Powers, 1780–1914* (London, 1981).
2. See, especially, R. Wade, *Governing the Market: Economic Theory and the Role of Government in East Asian Industrialisation* (Princeton, 1990).
3. World Bank, *The East Asian Miracle* (Oxford, 1993).

The State as Economic Engine:
Lessons from the Japanese Experience

CHARLES J. McMILLAN

I: JAPANESE POLITICAL ECONOMY

Japan is different. Japan is not a capitalist country, because it operates on the principle of a guided market-place. Bureaucrats set the rules, including those to keep foreigners at bay. So goes a key refrain of writers in Japan, among them Clyde Prestowitz, Chalmers Johnson, and Karel van Wolferen, who have written penetrating books on bureaucratic protectionism, industrial policy, and political dynamics in Japan.[1] The usual refrain is that Japan's historical evolution places its industrial structure outside the mainstream of advanced capitalist countries, as a mercantilist and protectionist economy against Western countries. The evidence for this debate is highly controversial in several respects. First, it is not clear what benchmark is used to analyse current policy through historical behaviour. Second, in most major advanced countries government plays a major role in the economy, employing specific instruments such as tax and investment, trade, environment, transportation and other policies. Third, all capitalist countries, including Japan, have started with a strong central role for government, from Jeffersonian America to Victorian Britain, from Bismarkian Germany to Meiji Japan. In the 1980s, the debate regarding Japan's industrial policy was framed mainly in terms of US–Japan relations, particularly trade and protectionism. In the 1990s, arguments focused on the advantages and disadvantages of Japan's 'mixed model' for application to other countries. Asia itself is the competitive playing field, as most of the Asian Tigers, adopting models similar to Japan's export-led growth, are applying manufacturing technologies equal to anything used in the West. More recently, the break-up of the Soviet Union has forced the emerging republics to set up new institutions, based on models from the West. Some republics have looked to Japan and the export-led model of Asia. So this debate has become more academic. Countries as diverse as China and the former Republics of the Soviet Union in central Asia – for example, Kazakhstan and Kyrghystan – are adopting Japanese approaches to market reform and state-led industrial development.

Analysts differ about the role of the Japanese government in the economy partly because they lack clear benchmarks. Curiously, classical

Charles J. McMillan, York University, Toronto

economics provides no theory or model on this important question, except at the two extremes of a total market economy (which does not exist in any advanced country) and a total 'command' economy (which exists only in fully totalitarian states). Thus, on any basic quantitative index, such as the percentage of government activity in the total GNP, or the level of tax spending, there is no simple correlation with economic performance. High spending Sweden is not appreciably different from low spending Switzerland; West Germany scores close to the USA.[2] Indeed, between the extremes of *laissez-faire* Hong Kong and the centralist institutions of China and the former Communist bloc countries of the Soviet Union, Japan and Western nations including the USA have a long tradition of government involvement in the economy. France is the best example: its *dirigiste* model of industrial and financial control was instituted by Colbert at the time of Louis XIV; it extends to the centralising initiatives of Napoleon and continues to the state ownership model of post-war de Gaulle and the socialists under Francois Mitterrand after 1981. Two centuries ago, in his *Lettres Anglaises*, Voltaire contrasted France's experience with the Anglo-Saxon libertarian brand of commerce – a difference underscored by the Reagan–Thatcher ideological activism in the USA and Britain in the 1980s. Reagan and Thatcher sought to reduce government's role primarily in such areas as deficits, regulations, state ownership and taxes. Japan has remained largely outside this debate, despite the empirical evidence that it is the one country that practises capitalist non-intervention and limits the role of government. What is different is how government in Japan assures certain fundamentals: it manages strategic vulnerabilities, especially the lack of energy and raw materials; develops competitive technologies; and fosters social harmony, by for example ensuring equality before the law and relatively equal income. Japan's top 20 per cent of income earners make only three times that of the bottom 20 per cent, compared to nine times in the USA. Traditionally, the major government levers used in the capitalist economies have been in three categories: broad stabilisation policies within a Keynesian framework; monetary policy affecting interest rates, inflation, and the value of the currency; and defence policy. In recent years, the trends towards international competition and competitive rivalry have added a new dimension to the government's role, namely industrial strategy-making or planned industrial development to shape comparative advantage.[3]

II: THE STATE AS ECONOMIC FIGURE

The view of Japan Incorporated (or Japan Inc.) – although three decades old – is still held by many adherents amongst foreigners, both in the public at large and in Washington. True there was a certain measure of historic truth in the idea. Certainly by comparison with the United States, the Japanese government through key ministries had a far larger role to play than equivalent or near equivalent ministries in Washington or London. Moreover, there is an enormous difference in the approach to business–government relations, which in Japan involves constant and quite detailed levels of interaction between executives in the corporate sector and the government ministries, and amongst low level officials too, in an attempt to reach overall consensus on a coherent and long-range vision of the forward direction of the economy. By contrast, the US typically displays almost no coherence across government departments, constant turnover of key officials, treatment of major domestic economic issues in isolation from foreign policy issues, and virtually no high-level bureaucratic apparatus to link trade and investment policies to domestic programmes and policies. Consequently, there can be some appreciation of Patrick and Rosovsky's observation that, for Japan, 'the nature and extent of the government–business relationship is in many respects similar to that in France, West Germany, and other continental European nations; the United States is perhaps the atypical case'.[4] The parallels between Japan and Western countries in terms of the state's role in economic development are actually much closer to Europe's aristocratic traditions than the US model.[5] Unlike the US legacy of a Madison-style division of powers and factions of minorities, Japan's post-Meiji government was headed by an emperor who 'was simultaneously head of state, head of government, highest lawgiver, supreme judge, and commander in chief of all armed forces'.[6] Absolutism was the form of government during the formative years of Japan's market economy; the absolutism turned to militarism, which in defeat changed to an imposed democracy.

When the major choices for economic development were made in the last century, the national slogan, 'Fukoku Kyohei' – rich country and strong army – was reflected in the government institutions at large. Because the actual choices for emulating foreign countries were not great – capitalist in North America or Europe, where the image of national richness originated – the role of the merchant class and the new bureaucracy quickly became apparent. The state machinery of samurai administrators built a web of enterprises and institutions tied to the 'political merchants', who joined forces with the government while letting the state take many of the social risks. Social ideologies based around nationalism and a type of manifest destiny provided a form of social glue with the masses, even though the bureaucracy operated on the feudal principle of 'Kanson Minpi' – revere the official, despise the common man. The basis of Japan's institutional character up to the end of 1945 was firmly in place for two generations. The large and efficient industrial sector, supported by government and exploited by the political merchants, contrasted with the position of the agricultural and light industry sectors.

While the economy itself was developing a modern merchant and entre-
preneurial class, the government was dominated by a traditional and self-
serving bureaucracy, which increasingly merged its own interests with
imperialistic militaristic adventures. As Boulding and Gleason have
pointed out, there was a basic continuity between the Pacific War aims of
the 1940s and Japan's movements in Asia from the Meiji period:

> the Meiji government, once isolationism had been abandoned,
> resumed the imperialistic practices of an earlier era. The policy of
> expansion was supported by a powerful traditional, nationalistic
> sentiment or pride which rested on the belief that the Japanese were
> a nation divinely established and favoured, a kind of chosen people
> of the Orient, destined to rule the less favoured.[7]

The high level of centralisation in the economy, and the general attempt
to mobilise resources for government-imposed goals, such as imperialism
in the decade up to the Pacific War and the war itself, shaped not only the
institutional character of the government but left a legacy of values,
attitudes, and even language among the bureaucrats and their subordinates. The result was a surprising level of continuity between the pre-
war years and the post-war years: during the occupation years, the level of
government control was unparalleled. Chalmers Johnson, the leading
proponent of Japan's state capitalist development, goes so far as to
argue that the pre-war experience was not entirely negative for post-war
economic development:

> The experience of the 1930s and 1940s was not by any means
> totally negative for post-war Japan; these were the years in which
> the managerial tools of the developmental state were first tested,
> some being rejected and others proving useful. Overcoming the
> depression required economic development, war preparation and
> war fighting required economic development, post-war reconstruc-
> tion required economic development, and independence from US
> aid required economic development. The means to achieve develop-
> ment from one cause ultimately proved to be equally good for the
> other causes.[8]

Foreign interpretations of the Japanese political system emphasise two
themes: the powerful role of the state, in particular key ministries like
MITI, and the elite role of the key bureaucrats. Clearly, this picture is
incomplete. In general terms, it is a description that could equally apply
to other successful post-war countries, as diverse as France and Canada.
Such a view ignores the fundamental role of politics, political competition,
the media, and political values, including the changing political culture of
Japan during a process of internationalisation. It ignores the activist role
of governments in international trade policy and technological develop-

ment – the new battleground of international economics in the global market-place. Industrial planning in Japan is the judicious mixture of government intervention usually associated with a socialist economy, the jawboning and cajoling usually seen in the American economy, and the long-range vision normally recognised as characteristic of good management. At the heart of the country's industrial planning is the view of the total economy as a portfolio of sectors, many interrelated and interdependent, each having specific features such as energy intensity, technological sophistication, export orientation, and the like. The term 'industrial structure' is the Japanese phrase used to explain this concept, and various government white papers provide detailed statistical analysis of its evaluation, direction, and implications for the domestic economy.

The conceptual underpinnings of Japan's post-war growth had many influences; not the least was the experience of total industrial devastation and military defeat. In this real world, similar in some ways to that of the CIS countries of the former Soviet Union, bureaucrats and businessmen had few intellectual anchors to guide them, since there was so little parallel with previous experience. Japan's history, it must be remembered, did not draw on the liberal political traditions of Anglo-Saxon democracy – the nationalism and non-interventionist ideas of Adam Smith and later David Ricardo, and the precepts of free trade and open markets. Germany was much more influential in Japan's intellectual foundations, notably the school of economics identified with Frederick List (1787–1846), whose major work, *National System of Political Economy*, was published in 1841. List, who travelled widely, including to the USA and England, and suffered persecution for his unorthodox views and experienced jail and exile, was one of the first institutional economists to develop a stages model of economic development. From the primitive and pastoral stages, national economies, according to List, moved from agricultural, agricultural–manufacturing, to agricultural–manufacturing–commercial – the high point symbolised by England's advanced stage at the time of his writings. List identified the role of the state as a critical vehicle to advance the nation state to more advanced stages, arguing, for example, for the need for a customs union for the German states (the *Zollverein*) and the construction of German railroads. He proposed the use of 'educational tariffs' to increase the productive capacity of the economy, despite the costs involved, and as a necessary step before moving to the advanced stage of open trade and full development characteristic of England's commercial economy.[9] Japanese economists and policy makers have been heavily influenced by the institutional, nation-building role found in such writers as List and many others. Japan's post-war reconstruction was built on such ideas. Where the lessons of Anglo-Saxon economics have been strongest – in, for instance, the Friedmanite ideas of personal freedoms and market choice, and the macro, Keynesian models of market stabilisation – the Japanese have added the German traditions symbolised by Frederick List, and picked up by such writers as diverse as W.W. Rostow's *Stages of Economic Growth* and Gunnar Myrdal's *The Political Element in the Development of Economic Theory*.[10]

III: THE JAPAN INC. MODEL

Outside Asia, understanding of Japan's industrial system is rather low and superficial. The stereotype image of Japan Inc. is well ingrained. The element of truth derives from success, not the causes. This pattern is reinforced in the media by such well-publicised issues as Nippon Telephone and Telegraph's intransigence on foreign sourcing, or the government's well-known efforts at protecting domestic agriculture, especially rice imports.[11] Japan is the most 'calorie-supply' dependent country in the industrialised world, reflecting both high population density and limited arable land – 14 per cent of the total, of which 56 per cent is devoted to rice paddies. Behind these issues are two critically important concerns. The first is the complex relationships between the farmers and the web of agricultural co-ops and related agricultural federations (*noyko*) which have acted in close concert with the Department of Agriculture and, through it, the Liberal Democratic Party. Japan's farmers thus have enormous influence in Japanese politics, affecting, for example, land reform and subsidy support for rice and other products, and distorting labour and consumption patterns, particularly between rural and urban Japan. The second issue relates to Japan's increasing multilateral obligations to international trade initiatives, where a main agricultural proposal is tariffication, or turning non-tariff barriers into an openly exposed tariff regime of progressively diminished barriers. Reinforcing this squeeze on Japan's agricultural protection is the steadily rising value of the yen, which makes agricultural imports in such areas as grains, vegetables, and meats vastly more competitive. Changing consumption patterns in Japan – grain versus rice, meats versus fish – provide domestic impetus to the decline of Japanese agriculture, with enormous consequences for the post-war political system and Japan's traditional diet and health standards.

Analytically, however, Japan's industrial planning is considerably more complex. It is also more sophisticated. For one thing, the planning exercise is not one of creating fixed blueprints of a static industrial structure, as planning critics often argue.[12] The major body responsible for developing and deliberating on industrial structure, the Industrial Structure Council (*Sangyo Kozo Shingrikai*, or *Sankashin* in brief), is actually an advisory body of a cross-section of well-informed industrial, academic, financial, bureaucratic and trade union leaders. The chairman of the council is the head of the *Keidanren* and there are 130 authorised members who serve renewable two-year terms. A second consideration is that there is virtually no ideological component to the planning process, at least in the sense of being 'capitalist' or 'socialist'.[13] Planning, of course, is a highly loaded term. In recent years, elections have been fought on the role of government in Canada, Britain, Sweden, France and the United States. In Japan, business–government relations are not governed by such ideological overtones, at least not until the 1993 election when campaign spending became a central issue. It is for this reason that a general societal consensus is probably easier to mould on the broad thrust of Japan's industrial structure, especially given global changes, technology and political trends. The conceptual basis of Japan's evolution has focused on industrial structure around heavy industrial goods, or *jukagaku kogyoko*. The main beneficiaries of these policies were in the heavy machinery, chemical and machine tool sectors, where high income elasticity of demand prevailed. In this situation, as world income levels increased with more global trade, demand for Japanese goods via exports became even higher. The forward direction of Japan's industrial structure is a service-oriented, knowledge-based economy based on micro-electronics, biotechnology and new raw materials. This approach, called *chisiki sangyo*, is a response to the ever upward revaluation of the yen, rising energy prices, the terms of trade for raw materials, land shortages and rising costs, and pollution abatement. The aim is to move away from sectors which are land-intensive, pollution-intensive, and energy-intensive (the so-called *keiretsu* sectors such as steel, shipbuilding, and chemicals) into high value-added knowledge sectors (computers, electronics, fashion, leisure, pharmaceuticals, fine chemicals, and the like). Japan, in short, is moving to the knowledge-intensive service economy, although not as fast or as thoroughly as the United States. Japan's service economy is important in several respects. First, it is tangible evidence that Japan's future is largely on the same path as other Western economies, away from the manufacturing of traditional products, especially heavy industry, and oriented to high value-added, knowledge-intensive products. Second, Japan's adjustment to global competitiveness and international trade has reinforced the domestic momentum towards increasing emphasis on a host of new industry and corporate strategies, many of which will impact service sectors in the world economy. Examples include medical services, education, leisure and sports, engineering and construction, travel and tourism, multimedia, financial services, communications and transportation. Third, the Japanese increasingly recognise that the management demands of the smokestack sectors of heavy manufacturing, exemplified by iron ore, steel, shipbuilding, automobiles, machinery and petrochemicals, no longer represent the future job opportunities for the international dimension of the global economy. Their place has been taken by the airlines, financial services, communications, fashion and

clothing, leisure, health and automation sectors in all their forms. The
scramble for international partnerships, strategic alliances and joint
ventures is under way in a massive fashion. The Japan of the 1990s is a far
cry from the energy-dependent, technology-follower Japan of the 1970s.

Another interpretation of Japan's performance was best set out by
Herman Kahn in his popular book, *The Emerging Japanese Superstate*.[14] In
his view, economic, social, and psychological factors combine to give Japan
unique performance growth rates: only time awaits the point when Japan's
economy overtakes the USSR and later the US, to be what Vogel predicted
in *Japan As No.1*.[15] Surprisingly, however much the Japanese enjoyed
and read the foreign comments on Japan's success and future status, as
witnessed by the best selling books on the subject, few Japanese really
believed that the country was anywhere near the apex of the economic
pecking-order, especially citizens in the large cities of Tokyo and Osaka.
No country in the world, at least during the last 25 years, has so correctly
perceived the dynamics of the international economy, including the
emergence of labour-intensive Third World economies, as has Japan.[16] As
a consequence of this realistic assessment of world trading patterns,
Japan has oriented its domestic manufacturing mix with a specific orientation to the global patterns of trade and foreign investment. Even though
exports comprise one of the lowest percentages of GNP of any major
Western nation – 10–11 per cent of GNP, compared to 8–9 per cent in the
US, 25 per cent in Canada and Britain, and 40 per cent in West Germany
– in manufacturing alone, the Japanese rate is about 50 per cent. The
planning of industrial structure outlined above relates directly to the
country's export strategy. The composition of exports is not entirely
identical to the domestic mix of the manufacturing sector, for two reasons.
First, for many products such as colour televisions, exports from Japan
actually preceded the growth in production for the domestic market, a fact
which reflected the differences in incomes and consumer tastes between
foreign markets and Japan. Second, Japan is capable of relating the level
of exports to domestic demand such that by long production runs of fairly
specific products, like watches, huge productivity gains are possible which
allow entry and penetration of foreign markets even as domestic demand
is growing. By contrast, in many Western countries, export growth occurs
after domestic market saturation has been reached.[17]

The dynamics of Japan's export strategy is a realistic national economic
strategy of continually shifting into higher value-added, high productivity
sectors, and, of course, exiting from industries which do not meet these
criteria. The impact of these changes provides the basis for understanding
not only the restructuring of Japan's domestic market, but also the new
division of labour taking place in the enormous Asian market at large.
The planning behind these structural adjustments are typically related to
two additional considerations at firm-level in Japan. First, by adding

export potential to domestic production growth concurrently, rather than in a step-wise fashion of many Western competitors, Japanese firms have gained enormous productivity advantages from scale economies. In many sectors, Japanese firms are unrivalled for building optimal scale plants.[18] Second, by recognising the managerial and labour advantages from fast growth, Japanese firms accumulate the economics of learning and experience curves. Very fast growth can mean spectacular improvements in per unit costs as output increases. The cost–volume relationship, often depicted as progress–cost curves, means that savings can be as much as 30 per cent or more with a doubling of output. These are the process engineering issues which provide competitive companies, regardless of location or ownership, with the new tools for the winning edge.[19] Japan's penchant for gathering and collecting statistics is well known. One very important role such statistics can serve is to distinguish between sectors with falling demand or temporary dislocation problems (for example, the need to invest in new machinery) and sectors with fundamental structural problems of obsolete technology, declining productivity, or uncompetitive cost position. More than in most countries, Japan has been able to identify these sectors, to recognise the difference between short run and long run difficulties, and to reallocate resources away from sunset sectors to sunrise sectors. A report prepared on the United States–Japan trade by the Comptroller General put the difference starkly:

> In comparing US and Japanese trade policies, [we find] the sharpest contrast in the different approaches toward export industries. Japan's commercial policy rests on identifying industries with strong potential and providing them with support. In the United States there is no analysis of export potential among industries. Shoes and computers are regarded equally. Before targeting an 'export industry', Japan asks 'Do the products of this industry have a high value added content? Will the demand for this product rise with rising income?' These questions are not asked in the United States. Japan encourages its strong industries; the United States protects its weak ones.

Declining industries are sectors where there is a sustained absolute decrease in unit sales and where lower cost imports threaten a permanent challenge for cost competitiveness.[20] Individual firms have a mixture of strategic options in the face of a declining industry environment, such as the selection of market niches, controlled disinvestment, or quick liquidation. The significance of the Japanese approach to sunset sectors is, however, a pervasive willingness to face up to the dislocation costs of uncompetitive industrial sectors and to develop a planning approach to long term decline. How is this planning function carried out?

The two major bureaucratic players in this exercise are the Industrial

Structure Council and MITI. Japan's Fair Trade Commission is rather weak and does not have the communications links of other government units. MITI bureaucrats work from comparative growth statistics and import data to analyse the underlying cost structure of raw material, production, technology and the like to ascertain the degree of severity of a sunset sector's competitive disadvantage. Once a sector is targeted as a lame duck, the signals in the business community are quickly picked up and a rather typical pattern develops. The first move is to reduce industry capacity, often in staged cuts. In the aftermath of the second energy crisis in 1979, this pattern has been in force in aluminium smelting, synthetic fibres, oil refining, steel, petrochemicals, shipbuilding, chemical fertilisers, and paper, to cite examples. Cuts in capacity are closely linked to market share and production rates – between 1976 and 1981, as one prominent instance, the top five steel producers maintained output of crude steel at exactly the same share of total output. The costs of cuts in capacity are borne first by the companies involved and by tariff revenues. The cost of shifting capacity out of coal-mining was covered in part by a ten per cent duty on petroleum imports. More recently, where MITI forced a reduction in aluminium smelter capacity, tariffs on imported ingots were used to pay for the structural adjustment period. Outright cartels – industry cooperation on such fundamental issues as production volume, pricing, inventories and sales agreements – are permissible under the law;[21] for example, this approach has been widely used in shipbuilding and in steel. In some cases, import controls may be permitted, especially when modernisation of equipment with new technology or energy savings may signal a return to profitability. However, such instances have been quite rare in the post-war period; import controls really signal a prelude to long-term decline. A related response is to specialise in high value-added areas, even if the market niche is limited or involves export development. The third move involves a reallocation of workers. Policies which are key to this approach involve subsidised retraining programmes, early retirement of older workers, movement of labour into other sectors or to other business units of the bigger corporations. In the post-war period, generally strong economic growth has allowed this reallocation approach to work well, and there has been limited union resistance to shifting employment because lay-offs have usually been seen as the last managerial response to competitive decline.

The underlying processes of decision-making for declining sectors are identical to sunrise sectors. At the most general level, there is an enormous statistical basis for major decisions; there is also a constant interplay of communciations, lobbying, cajoling, and industrial gamesmanship. On the government side, there is not only the pressure of individual politicians, representing declining industry prefectures, but the *Gen Kyoku* or 'original bureau' responsible for each industry sector.

Their institutional counterpart in the private sector are the hundreds of trade associations representing specific industrial interests. Both sides hold constant and elaborate meetings and consider a wide range of such issues as technology, tariff policy, tax law, imports, and foreign investment. There may well be sharp disagreement between both sides on some issues, such as, for example, the timing of import liberalisation.[22] However, judged by the reduction in relative importance of major sectors in the Japanese economy over the past two decades, and the emerging prominence of new sectors such as electronics, life sciences, and new materials, Japan's approach to sunset industries can be seen as a costly but ruthless recognition of comparative disadvantage in the industrial structure. The Japanese experience demonstrates how the route for declining industries may not be a closing down of a business unit but one of shifting production via foreign investment to offshore markets where comparative advantage is higher. The idea is to shift the production site from Japan where unit costs are too high to a foreign site where input costs are lower than the domestic industry structure. The pattern is not only eminently rational from the point of view of Japan's industrial evolution; it usually means as well that Japanese foreign investment complements the trade characteristics of the host country. Much of Japan's first foreign investment took place in South East Asia, usually in the form of joint ventures, in sectors such as textiles and cutlery where the opportunities for low-cost production were greater than onshore. This process is now being extended to include high wage countries like the United States and western Europe, because of their domestic comparative advantage in labour and raw materials supplies. For the domestic economy, this approach has two major consequences. First, by the process of 'throw away' industries, the economy allocates its main resources to sectors where Japan has comparative advantages, now or in the future. There is considerably less pressure to prop up lame-duck industries where there is no hope of salvage. Second, the shift of the domestic industrial structure towards high value-added means that each sector feeds on the improvements and developments in other sectors. For example, large-scale firms promote the sophisticated products or processes into small firms; consumer industries are spurred by the new equipment processes developed by the industrial goods sectors. The overall impact is for the major sectors of the economy to develop a momentum by the major actors – and for managers, workers, and government officials to understand Japan's basic direction and ruthlessly assess performance on relative growth and productivity.

IV: JAPANESE LESSONS

The planning process for developing Japan's industrial structure has no parallel either in the mixed market economies of the West or the planned economies of the communist regimes. Ironically, while many Western observers would suggest that Japan is indeed a unique case, the fact is that Japan is the model of most of the countries of South East Asia. Both these countries and Japan share an economic feature not readily perceived in the West, namely that while a planning process is in force, buttressed by strong business–government relations, they are all Friedmanite economies where governments account for less than 30 per cent of GNP, or, in some cases, no more than half that of the capitalist USA. The main point of Japan's economic planning is not to produce a blueprint. It is to give direction, and that direction is clearly market- and trade-oriented. For Western countries, there is a constant lag in perceptions of what Japan is doing. There can be no question that in years past Japan has used all kinds of trade and non-trade barriers to keep imports at bay and foreign investment to a minimum. Moreover, there are still some sectors which remain protectionist and inward looking, agriculture being the prime example. Yet it is another matter to generalise the workings of the entire economy on the basis of these specific examples. It is equally misleading to ignore the future path of Japan's industrial structure based on the pattern of exports in the 1960s and early 1970s. Japan is well past the stage of post-war reconstruction and needs no government props to remain technologically and industrially competitive.

Contrary to evidence from planning sceptics, the Japanese model serves a very useful purpose, namely the educational function of clarifying past mistakes and future options. In this respect, Japan's approach is ruthlessly performance-oriented, and acts as a barometer against international standards. Countries in South East Asia have started to emulate Japan's analytical techniques to design their evolving industrial structures and, indeed, in a number of instances they are now severely threatening many once competitive sectors such as consumer electronics, computers, and advanced office equipment. However, the particular features of the new industrialising countries of South East Asia – their geographical proximity to Japan, their capacity to buy catch-up technology, their transportation advantages – are quite different from the major economies of North America and western Europe. Japan's success has prompted a public debate on the relative merits of industrial planning, even in the United States. Most of this discussion has taken on the flavour of highly charged ideological overtones. France has become the one Western country most obsessed with Japanese-style industrial planning, and has studied the approach in some detail, but from a vantage-point in the 1960s of direct intervention and state ownership. Despite the attention given to the Japanese model, most foreign observers fail to recognise why, at bottom, the system has been successful. For one thing, there is limited recognition of the incredibly thorough discussions and information exchange between industry and government. A typical description of this dialogue is explained in cultural terms of conformity and consensus, but too little appreciation is given to the efforts of both sides to achieve a competitive industrial structure. A related point is that while the Japanese plan, the industrial sector is fiercely market-oriented. There is little sympathy for the view usually found in Europe of picking a single industrial champion for each sector: the Japanese approach is akin to a stable of race horses – a stable with many champions competing in each racing category. Despite being half the size of the USA, Japan has more companies in almost all key sectors, a point recognised by Porter.[23] The elaborate set of government levels for industry – tariffs, foreign investment controls, government procurement, tax policies, and financial loans – are all geared to an optimal industrial structure which is globally competitive. The competitive difficulties of many European industries in their own markets is a measure of the ineffectiveness of excessive reliance on state planning, protection, and state ownership.

One additional issue is the Japanese obsession with technology as a key to industrial productivity. Value-added has been a recurrent theme of the planning approach and the underlying rationale for growth in some sectors and not others. Japanese dependence on foreign resources and foreign technology have reinforced the desire for an effective national response. The model of industrial structure planning has several decades of practice and the decision-making processes between business and the government and internal to the corporation or the bureaucracy reinforce it. Japan's economy, it must be remembered, is firmly anchored in a society where trust, personal relationships, and team cooperation are highly coveted. Market competition is not viewed as a mechanism to take advantage of the next person or company regardless of social cost, and, unlike the United States, contractual obligations are as much about personal relations as anything backed up by an army of lawyers. In this sense, Japan's huge array of networks – business–government, business–university, company–supplier, company–workers – minimise transaction costs, the ebb and flow of decisions, incentives, and information in markets. Money incentives are important, but so too are issues like cooperation, trust and non-material rewards. Much of the foreign analogies with industrial planning in Japan are either mistaken or misplaced. In terms of the overall economy, the role of the government – or specific departments like MITI – is vastly overrated, especially after the Nixon shock of 1971, when the yen started a steady path of upward revaluation. Where the government does have a role, the clear lesson for Western countries is one of maximum co-ordination of effort – for example, tax policies, manpower programmes, R&D support, and regional policy. Japan's resource dependence and export trade consciousness heavily reinforce this coordinated effort.

A second lesson is that Japanese industrial planning is most influential at the two extremes of the industrial sector – in emerging sunrise sectors or the declining sunset sectors. While the government's role is clearly influential, it is by no means blindly supportive to corporate interests when competitiveness is low. Unlike most European countries, the Japanese government rigorously promotes strong, indeed ferocious, competition in each sector by assuring several market entrants. Japan's competing *keiretsu* groups reinforce this industrial rivalry. In sunset sectors, the government's success has largely been due to careful co-ordination of the various levers in the policy arsenal. Because the planning approach is fundamentally microeconomic in nature, the basic differences across sectors can be learned, assessed, studied, and acted on. In the United States, for instance, most government programmes for ailing industries are not coordinated and many policies are macroeconomic in nature. As a 1991 *Business Week* report on the US economy noted:

> Relying solely on microeconomic policies is not likely to solve the problem of sectoral fragmentation now confronting the US. Instead government policies will have to be carefully targeted to meet special needs. The requirements of ailing basic technologies are obviously different than those of the energy and high-technology industries.

A third lesson with Japan's approach is the continual commitment to analyse significant global economic and technological trends and their impact on the domestic economy. Corporations and trading firms do this in Japan, of course, but certain national objectives – energy, trans-portation, housing, food, and education – can only be met by government input. Some work undertaken by MITI has American counterparts in the defence and space programmes in the United States, but the US approach is piecemeal and fragmented, partly because this need is not publicly admitted. This constant monitoring of Japan's relative position, publicised in an endless array of statistical sources, greatly increases the public aware-ness of economic and trade issues and makes for informed public policy. The point also underscores the important role of technology planning by governments and corporations alike, across the technology cycle, through pre-competitive and competitive technological development.

NOTES

1. See C.V. Prestowitz, *Trading Places: How We Allowed the Japanese to Take the Lead* (New York, 1988); C. Johnson, *MITI and the Japanese Miracle* (1982).
2. Samuelson (1980).
3. A decade ago, the literature on industrial strategy was small. In the 1990s, virtually all countries have an industrial policy industry, in government, academe, and consulting. See M.E. Porter, 'Industrial Policy', 6 April 1992; and J.M. Fallows, *Looking at the Sun: The Rise of the New East Asian Economic and Political System* (1994).
4. H. Patrick and M. Rosovsky, *Asia's New Giant: How the Japanese Economy Works* (1976). The duplication of effort and lack of departmental coordination prompted President Bill Clinton to establish a New Economic Council, modelled on the National

Security Council, to bring order in departments with mandates for international trade policy: State, Treasury, Agriculture, Defense, Commerce, Labor, Transportation, and Energy.
5. K. Nakagawa, *Government and Business* (Tokyo, 1980) traces Japan's business–government relationship, as compared to Britain, Germany, and the US.
6. Sumiya and Taira (1979), p.191.
7. Boulding and Gleason (1972), p.247.
8. Johnson, *MITI*, p.308.
9. F. List, *National System of Political Economy* (1841).
10. W.W. Rostow, *Stages of Economic Growth* (1960); Gunnar Myrdal, *The Political Element in the Development of Economic Theory* (1953).
11. Kakurai (1993) and Egaitsu (1993). For an excellent overview from the perspective of a major agricultural exporter to Japan, see Riethmuller (1988).
12. Sharpe (1975).
13. Chie Nakane, in an interview in *Newsweek*, 15 Oct. 1973, p.60 makes the point as follows: 'The Japanese way of thinking depends on the situation rather than principle – while with the Chinese it is the other way around. The Chinese are the people who developed the classics and can't do anything without principle. But we Japanese have no principles. Some people think we hide our intentions, but we have no intentions to hide. Except for some few leftists or rightists, we have no dogma and don't ourselves know where we are going'. See C. Nakane, *Japanese Society* (1971).
14. H. Kahn, *The Japanese Emerging Superstate: Challenge and Response* (1970).
15. E. Vogel, *Japan as No. One: Lessons for America* (1973).
16. The social science literature suggests that countries, as well as corporations, develop institutional rigidities and policy paralysis, thereby leading to relative industrial decline. For countries, this means an isolation of government and self-serving bureaucracies, a plethora of one-issue interest groups, and an institutional bias towards the *status quo*, independent of performance. Note that this perspective is more complex and sophisticated than the more widely viewed reason for industrial decline, namely imperial overstretch and spending on defence beyond a country's financial and economic resources. For a work at the country level, see P. Kennedy, *The Rise and Fall of Great Powers: Economic Change and Military Conflict from 1500–2000* (1987). See also Huntington (1988). For a fascinating account at the corporate level, based on the leading auto firms, see Keller (1993).
17. In many sectors, Japanese producers have focused on particular niches, once abandoned (small, black and white televisions) or poorly developed (sporty motorcycles). By aggressive marketing and in too many cases by passive foreign rivalry, Japanese firms have quickly gained market share to reinforce their long production runs and resulting lower unit costs. The pattern becomes a reinforcing virtuous circle in favour of Japanese productivity.
18. Gold (1981), p.14.
19. Stalk (1992).
20. M.E. Porter, *Competitive Strategy* (Harvard, 1980), p.255 writes: 'Industries differ markedly in the way competition responds to decline; some industries age gracefully; whereas others are characterized by bitter warfare, prolonged excess capacity, and heavy operating losses. Successful strategies vary just as widely. Some firms have reaped high returns from strategies actually involving heavy reinvestment in a declining industry that make their businesses better cash cows later. Others have avoided losses subsequently borne by their competitors by exiting before the decline was generally recognised, and not harvesting at all'. For an examination of corporate strategies for declining industries, see Harrigan (1980).
21. According to a French study, 'The formation of cartels, authorised by MITI, in accord with the monopoly law, for treating particular industrial problems constitutes a very powerful tool of industrial policy. It is one of the keys of capacity adjustment of Japanese enterprises and what presents a common front in matters of industrial questions (exports and divisions of markets, investment, transfer of technology)'. J.-P. Souviron, *Strategie de Reponse au Defi Japonais* (Paris, 1981), p.22.
22. There has been a clear trend away from MITI's activist interventionist approach towards the arms length, market philosophy of the Ministry of Finance. As far back as the 1960s, there were two well publicised incidents which illustrate not only this contrasting government philosophy at the ministerial level but the conflict between MITI and

private sector firms. In 1962, in the Takushinho incident, MITI attempted to have legislation passed to promote mergers via tax measures in key sectors facing tariff liberalisation. The Ministry of Finance and private lending institutions fought this approach and won. Three years later, MITI attempted steel production cuts, only to be faced with strong opposition from Sumitomo Metals. MITI has since become the leading proponent of voluntary export restraints.

23. M.E. Porter, *The Competitive Advantages of Nations* (New York, 1990).

Economic Theory and Industrial Policy in East Asia

TAN KOCK WAH and JOMO K.S.

I: ECONOMIC LIBERALISM AND EAST ASIA

The recent resurgence of economic liberalism – most notably in the United States and the United Kingdom in the 1980s – has irreversibly undermined the earlier Keynesian (and Marxist) economic influences, which tended to favour government intervention to achieve policy objectives. As observed by Tobin, this 'counter revolution' – culminating in the development of New Classical Macroeconomics, fortified by the emergence of the Rational Expectations school –

> extends laissez-faire pretensions to macroeconomic theory and policy, which undermines the case for monetary and fiscal stabilisation policies that most economists, even those opposed to micro-economic interventions, had previously come to accept.[1]

With the disintegration of the old socialist bloc in the Soviet Union and eastern Europe, communism is widely seen to have failed. The claimed superiority of the market has been further reinforced by a shift in the remaining communist regimes – especially in the People's Republic of China – towards greater reliance on market forces. The erosion of western European and other welfare states – largely due to the post-war ascendance of social democracy – since the stagflation of the 1970s is widely seen to have further weakened the case for state intervention, even for redistributive purposes. The virtues of the market economy appear to have never been more strongly demonstrated and affirmed than by contemporary trends.

Pressures have also grown since the 1980s, especially with the debt crisis, for economic liberalisation in developing countries, with far-reaching consequences. Approval of structural adjustment loans – under the auspices of the World Bank, with IMF endorsement – to Africa, Asia and Latin America have become conditional on recipient economies conforming to the conditionalities imposed by the two Bretton Woods institutions. Some of these requirements have included the removal of government subsidies and price controls, the devaluation of currencies, wage cuts, public expenditure cuts, privatisation, the relaxation of foreign exchange controls, interest rate increases and other measures to promote a better climate for foreign investment.

Tan Kock Wah and Jomo K.S., University of Malaya

Basically, the neo-liberal position assumes and argues that neo-classical economic principles are universally valid, as relevant to Europe or North America, as to Africa, Asia and Latin America. Thus, development economics has been denounced as misleading and harmful, 'the invention of a set of theoretical curiosities by the dirigistes to supplant the market'. Hence, it has been claimed that 'the demise of development economics is likely to be conducive to the health of both the economics and the economies of developing countries'.[2] The emergence of the East Asian newly industrialising countries (NICs) was attributed to free market forces, while economic stagnation elsewhere was identified with market distortions due to government intervention.[3] We will examine the theories underpinning neo-liberal views, and see how well founded these propositions are with reference to stylised facts and evidence from East Asian late industrialising economies, namely South Korea, Taiwan and Japan during the 1950s and 1960s. We suggest that the state failure argument is tautological in that the market mechanism can always be said to be working improperly due to some kind of state intervention or other.[4] As failure can always be attributed to some sort of distortion, the theory can never indeed be proved wrong! This article aims to address these issues by looking more critically at the theories and evidence underlying the neo-liberal *laissez-faire* paradigm. It also incorporates some key findings of another growing stream of literature which emphasises the positive directive role of the state in Japan, South Korea and Taiwan.

II: THEORETICAL FOUNDATIONS OF THE NEO-LIBERAL PARADIGM

Efficient Allocation Of Resources

Contrary to the dominant economic development policy approach in the 1950s, 1960s and 1970s, which assigned the state a substantial role in developing the economy and emphasised capital formation as the main engine of growth, neo-liberals have underlined the efficient allocation of resources as the primary source of growth. They have emphasised the importance of getting prices 'right' and of promoting competitive, relatively undistorted markets. Their central thesis is that long-run growth and development will emerge from the attainment of short-run allocative efficiency. In their view, 'getting the prices right' is both a necessary and often a sufficient condition for maximising the long-term growth rate. As long as economies have stayed within the free market framework, economic growth is never a problem. The East Asian economies are hailed as exemplar economies that have adhered to these principles to achieve success. As James Reidel notes:

[The lessons are, above all, that] neo-classical economic principles are alive and well, and working particularly effectively in the East Asian countries. Once public goods are provided for and the most obvious distortions corrected, markets seem to do the job of allocating resources reasonably well, and certainly better than centralised decision making. That is evident in East Asia, and in most other parts of the developing and industrial world, and is after all the main tenet of neo-classical economics.[5]

The bedrock of the free trade doctrine seems to lie in the concept of comparative advantage. The neo-classical approach to international trade theory, the static Hecksher-Ohlin-Samuelson (H-O-S) model, shows that any two nations will be better off, in the sense of enjoying more, if they concentrate on those activities for which their costs are relatively, though not necessarily absolutely cheaper, in effect concentrating on producing goods with resources which are domestically abundant. Resources will then be allocated efficiently provided that international market forces are allowed to determine the relative prices of internationally tradable goods in the domestic economy. That requirement, in turn, calls for free trade or a close approximation to it, with low or no impediments to imports and with relative prices that give no more incentive to sell on the domestic market than to sell abroad.

But is the emphasis on promoting a relatively undistorted competitive market and, for that matter, the liberalisation efforts of the World Bank and IMF adequate in promoting sustainable growth in developing countries? It has been noted that:

> in its present state, trade theory provides little guidance as to the role of trade policy and trade strategy in promoting growth . . . There is nothing in theory to indicate why a deviation from the [market optimum] should affect the rate of economic growth.[6]

Indeed, economic theory is generally silent about the effect of trade liberalisation on economic growth. Moreover, the theoretical benefits of liberalisation are based on comparative statics and involve once and for all changes in national income.[7] There is also no presumption that liberalisation can raise the rate of growth over the medium to long run.[8] Stein has recently argued that the structural adjustment programme in Africa is likely to lead to de-industrialisation due to serious deficiencies in its rationale:

> The neo-classical approach is problematic. It is the product of the rational-deductive method which is the foundation of neo-classical economics. As a result, the process of investigation and recommendation is inverted since the causal effect is presupposed prior to determining the effective cause. As a result, the diagnosis of the

malaise is under determined, leaving out vital structural features which are likely to impede its implementation . . . While there are problems with the structure of industry in Africa, hoping the market will solve the difficulties is no substitute for developing an industrial policy . . . while [Hecksher–Ohlin–Samuelson] would have us believe there is a natural basis for comparative advantage that the market will indicate, others might argue that opportunities are created, not inherited.[9]

In fact, the prescription of economic liberalisation for the realisation of comparative advantage is a static proposition more concerned with the *status quo* or present situation than future potential and it does not give enough weight to the possibility of dynamic gains from short-term distortions, and the possibility of creating comparative advantage through rapid structural change for countries concerned with long-run development. As an Indonesian economist, Suhartono, put it:

The context of the problem facing the developing countries is fundamentally different from that addressed by static analysis: it is not one of merely adjusting the allocation of given resources more efficiently, but rather it is a question of how to accelerate economic and social development . . . In economic terms, the problem, involves an expansion in the production possibility frontier, not only a movement along it, through increasing productive capacities and through the productive employment of unutilized or under-utilized factors of production. Since from the point of view of the developing countries, the analysis for static gains addresses itself to the wrong question, it is not of particular relevance.[10]

Further as Rodan argues:

The more fundamental theoretical flaw of the neo-classical position, however, is that they attempt to disembody policy decisions from their social and political environments . . . Another weakness of the approach is that it fails to specify the contribution of the state to comparative advantage itself. Indeed, for these writers, comparative advantage takes on an existence outside the realms of the concrete; it is a condition or a law independent of actors themselves. According to this approach, actors can distort comparative advantage or help realise it, but they cannot actually create or define it. Such a position is rejected . . . it is argued that the state can and does play a major role in shaping comparative advantage – not just by reducing or increasing the cost of factors of production, but also by conditioning the socio-political environment in which these costs are realised and exploited. It [is] argued that comparative advantage is not a natural, abstract law, but a position in the market, which is determined by a variety of empirical factors, some of which the state is clearly able to define with positive results.[11]

Hence, neo-classical economics, being more prescriptive than descriptive, usually ignore or

> downplay the social, political and historical dimension of the concept of comparative advantage, and so error is invited in both the attribution of causality of comparative advantage and in more narrowly prescribing the limits within which developmental choices can be made.[12]

By focusing on short-run static efficiency and by disparaging the role of the state, medium- and long-term industrial strategies and planning are effectively discouraged.

Consistent with these arguments, Sraffian or neo-Ricardian trade theorists have also shown that comparative advantage does not arise naturally, but is governed by differences in technology, consumer preferences and determinants of wages and profits. In other words, it can be deliberately created by economic policies. Further, net losses can result from unmanaged trade, and the adjustments needed to translate comparative advantage into competitive advantage may not be smooth and automatic.[13] In fact, comparative advantage based on low wages may not be realised as 'there is always a physiological or political limit beyond which real wages cannot be reduced'.[14] Thus, the so-called comparative advantage may remain hidden and unrealised for a long time. Meanwhile, the 'capital debate' – which also puts the very foundation of neo-classical economics into question – has disastrous implications for the internal logic of the theory. For if factor abundance cannot be defined independently of factor prices, then the building block of the theory is put into serious question. According to Evans and Alizadeh, the observation that relatively low wages – leading to comparative advantage in labour-intensive commodities – is favourable to export-led growth no longer holds.

> Many propositions, which are taken as self-evident in the neo-classical discussion of the NICs, cannot be taken for granted. For example, the observation which derives from static H-O-S theory that an abundant endowment of labour relative to capital is the cause (*ceteris paribus*) of relatively low wages, leading to a comparative advantage in labour-intensive commodities, with favourable income distribution consequences for export-led growth, no longer holds. In the more complex heterogeneous capital world, one can only describe the characteristics of a trading equilibrium as being associated with the export of labour or capital-intensive commodities (in the two-factor case). Thus, even at the most abstract level, the

question of what causes comparative advantage is qualified in an important way.[15]

Although the causal mechanism linking liberalisation to growth is unclear, neo-liberal proponents claim that the record supports such a causal relationship. Some of the major studies that they rely upon to support their arguments have been the research carried out by Little, Scitovsky and Scott on trade and industrialisation; by Balassa and associates at the World Bank on the structure of protectionism; and by Krueger and Bhagwati on trade liberalisation experiences in developing countries.[16] The World Bank's 1981 *World Development Report* is also alleged to have provided cross-sectional evidence of the adverse effects of price distortions on economic growth, while the 1987 *World Development Report* made an attempt to demonstrate the virtues of 'outward-orientated' trade regimes for the growth of developing countries.[17] All these works are said to have demonstrated a positive causal relationship between a liberal trade regime and economic as well as export growth.

However, studies by other researchers have cast doubt on Balassa's conclusion that 'the evidence is quite conclusive: countries applying "outward oriented" development strategies had a superior performance in terms of exports . . . whereas countries with continued inward orientation encountered increasing difficulties'.[18] Contrary to the findings of the *World Development Report 1981*, Alizadeh and Evans' own analysis of the World Bank's economic and non-economic variables has shown that confidence in the effect of price efficiency on growth is misplaced.[19] As pointed out by Jenkins:

> Price distortions [found in *World Development Report 1981*] only explain about a third of the difference in growth rates between different countries, indicating that other factors too are significant . . . There are similar problems with World Bank evidence of links between outward orientation and growth. The strongly outward-oriented group of countries which performs so well consists only of South Korea and the two city states, Hong Kong and Singapore, and can hardly provide a model for other Third World countries with large agricultural sectors and rural populations. There are moderately outward-oriented countries such as Chile and Uruguay, where GNP per capita and manufacturing output have stagnated between 1973 and 1985, and inward-oriented economies, such as Cameroon, Nigeria and Indonesia where manufacturing has grown at more than 10% a year over the same period. It has also been noted that many of the strongly inward-oriented economies are amongst the least developed economies in the Third World, and that in recent years, the least developed countries have grown more slowly than the middle income countries. Thus, the apparent

relationship between growth and trade orientation may simply reflect their greater obstacles to growth faced by the poorest countries . . . Somewhat surprisingly, in the light of the neo-liberal emphasis on both low price distortions and outward orientation as factors explaining growth, there seems to be no consistent relationship between the two variables. Cameroon and the Philippines both have low price distortions, but are classified as inward-oriented, while Chile and Turkey both have high indices of distortion, but are regarded as outward-oriented.[20]

Also the classification of countries by 'outward' and 'inward' trade regimes yields dubious results. Colclough points out that:

Although [outward orientation] is referred to as a continuous variable (with the generally agreed conclusion amongst neo-liberals being: the more of it the better) in practise it appears in the analysis as a 'dummy', having four or five values, each of which is a composite of nominal protection, effective protection, and effective subsidies (Balassa and Associates 1982, chapter 3) or, in the case of *World Development Report 1987*, of effective protection, of the use of quantitative restrictions, of export incentives, and of the degree of exchange rate overvaluation. These variables are like apples and pears, very different, and cannot easily be added together. Determining the membership of country groups (each implying a similar degree of outward orientation) thus becomes as much a matter of judgement as of measurement.[21]

Another important shortcoming of these studies is the lack of theoretical and empirical discussion of the role of non-economic determinants, notably the relevance of government interventions in promoting trade and the importance of institutional and international settings in determining growth. These issues are usually sidestepped and not adequately discussed. Hence, the cross-country evidence relevant to neo-liberal trade and industrial policy prescriptions is by no means unambiguous. It cannot be invoked to justify the unrestricted play of market forces and government non-intervention in the economy.[22] At best, 'it can only support a cautious assessment of what a free trade approach can be expected to achieve for a broad cross-section of developing countries'.[23]

III: STATES DISTORT MORE THAN PROMOTE GROWTH?

Prescriptions on the Role of Government

In neo-liberal orthodoxy, the government is generally seen as inefficient and corrupt, damaging the performance of the national economy by taking on functions which are beyond the 'proper and appropriate' role of

government. Many neo-liberal economists would concede that markets –
for example, for technology development, manpower training, and credit
to small firms and exporters – may fail seriously, warranting government
intervention to offset these distortions. However, they deny that such
arguments justify a sectoral or industry-specific industrial policy. For
them the appropriate response (given no revenue constraint) would be to
intervene as closely as possible to the source of market failure rather than
by using trade distortions to overcome the market failure, preferring
subsidies to tariffs and tariffs to import controls, and 'thus minimising the
introduction of other by-product distortions which may impose production
and consumption costs'.[24] However, the neo-liberals contend that there
are few inherent failures and that existing market imperfections are often
due to government-induced policy errors, said to distort, rather than
promote the smooth functioning of the market. According to neo-liberal
thinking, though the market may not be perfect, the free working of
the market is nevertheless the best means of approximating it. Lal, for
instance, argues that '[t]here are few, if any, instruments of government
policy which are non-distortionary, in the sense of not inducing economic
agents to behave less efficiently in some respects . . . The best that can be
expected is second best'. He claims to give reasons, rooted in second best
theory, '. . . why, of the only feasible alternatives – a necessarily imperfect
planning mechanism and a necessarily imperfect market mechanism – the
latter is likely to perform better in practice', thereby justifying free
trade.[25] Yet the requirements of the second best optimal conditions are
not only notoriously complicated, requiring information well beyond the
realm of the feasible, so raising information costs, but the theory also
acknowledges that the removal of some but not all distortions does not
guarantee that the economy achieves higher allocative efficiency – the net
welfare effect of piecemeal reform cannot be known *a priori*. As the
argument goes, '[i]f there is net loss, it may be second best to do nothing',[26]
but this is misleading, as one can also infer that: 'if there is net gain, it may
be second best for the government to intervene'. Welfare economics does
not seem to oppose government intervention on this ground.

Meanwhile, the experiences of South Korea and Taiwan suggest that
the neo-classical standard ranking of trade policy instruments in the order
of least to most efficient (direct import controls, tariffs and subsidies)
aimed at the point of distortion is questionable. As Evans notes:

> The East Asian experience suggests that trade policy instruments
> cannot be ranked in these terms separately from the institutional
> context within which they were applied. For example, highly
> selective quantitative controls have always been important in the
> South Korean case. Yet, associated rent-seeking behaviour has not
> been dominant, partly because of the role of a strong national

development ideology in countering these effects . . . More potently, it appears that quantitative controls were often tied to crude incentives. Access to import licences, for example, was linked to the export performance of the firm. Thus, the state combined incentives with instruments of direct control to achieve its selective industrial policies, which tariffs alone could not attain. In such cases, the standard ranking of interventions cannot be sustained. Quantitative controls tied to incentives, however crude, may emerge as superior to tariffs precisely because they provide the instruments for implementing an efficient interventionist industrial strategy.[27]

With respect to the 'appropriate' role of government, Krueger argues that the government – as a non-market organisation – should not concentrate on those areas of activity in which it has no comparative advantage (such as manufacturing, credit regulation and foreign exchange markets), as this will divert scarce government resources from those areas of activity (maintenance of law and order, provision of infrastructure and large-scale public services) which it has an advantage in undertaking.[28] More specifically, in the neo-liberal view, the essential economic functions of government should be very limited. According to Chowdhury and Islam, these should be limited to the following functions:

1. The state should primarily rely on market based, private-sector-driven initiatives in the mobilisation and allocation of resources to growth promoting activities;
2. The state should intervene only in cases of clearly established 'market failure' (that is, in cases where private sector operations do not correspond to societal interests);
3. Even in cases of proven market failure, the appropriate policy responses should be parametric measures (such as lump-sum-taxes and subsidies) as well as incentives that establish a private market (such as a venture capital market);
4. The state should provide 'pure public goods' (law and order, national defence, public infrastructure) including the proper assignment and enforcement of property rights;
5. The state should provide a stable and predictable macroeconomic environment through appropriate coordination of fiscal, monetary and exchange rate policies;
6. The state should adopt a free trade (or almost free trade) regime as a core component of a neutral policy regime.

A state which takes on functions beyond those stated above is said to be doing too much – taking on functions beyond the normal and proper functions of government, especially in the sphere of production.

In fact, the 'overactive' state is alleged to have contributed to the decline of the economies of developing countries. The 1981 *World Development Report* claims that 'the public sector is over-extended . . . which has resulted in slower growth than might have been achieved with available resources, and accounts in part, for the current crisis'. The 1987 *World Development Report* is equally pessimistic:

> The performance of state-owned enterprises varies widely between countries, but their record has frequently been poor, particularly in developing countries. They have clearly failed to play the strategical role in industrialisation that governments had hoped for. Financial rates of return have generally been lower for the state-owned enterprises than for the private sector, as recent comparative studies for Brazil, India, and Israel have indicated. Financial profitability has often been compromised by price control, but the indications are that the state-owned enterprises have also had a generally poor record of social profitability. They have often put large burdens on public budget and external debt.

However, the allegations that public enterprises are invariably inefficient or that most of them perform badly must be seriously qualified on both theoretical and empirical grounds. Ajit Singh has contended that there is no unambiguous empirical evidence that suggests pervasive inefficiency or the poor relative performance of public enterprises.[29] As pointed out by Colclough,

> the empirical evidence does not support this contention. There is no significant difference between the proportion of GDP accounted for by public spending in Sub-Saharan African countries (the region about which the above generalisation was made) and those in other parts of the world; nor is the functional breakdown of public spending significantly different. Equally, amongst SSA countries there is no apparent relationship between GDP growth rates achieved and the proportional importance of public spending. A recent, more comprehensive study shows that across the world, government size is positively associated with economic growth performance. This is so in the overwhelming majority of country cases (more than 100 time-series regressions), especially in developing countries.[30]

Thus, ironically,

> [t]he neo-liberals can point to numerous examples of the negative effects of state intervention in Third World countries. They deny the need for state intervention beyond the minimal requirements for the functioning of the market and the provision of certain public goods, and they ignore examples of positive results from state intervention. However, they can produce no clear evidence that countries

in which government spending is a relatively small proportion of GDP grew faster than those with high levels of state expenditure.[31]

Quite amazingly, however, in spite of the lack of supporting evidence, the desirability of achieving a reduction of state spending in developing countries has become one of the major themes of orthodox reform programmes, culminating in calls for privatisation and deregulation.

The Principal-Agent Problem And Self-Seeking Bureaucrats in Public Enterprises

Theoretically, there can be no *a priori* presumption that public enterprises are inherently less efficient than private firms. In the case of public enterprises, the argument normally arises in the context of the 'principal-agent' problem, where the principals (the public) are said to be in no position to monitor the performance and to contain the consequences of self-seeking behaviour by agents (public enterprise managers) due to the difficulty in acquiring the necessary information and in exerting influence on decision making. The inability of the public to rely on the government as 'agent' to effectively monitor the performance of public enterprise managers is often invoked as justification to curtail 'over-extended' public enterprises and to justify privatisation in order to achieve the supposedly more effective delegation structure of private firms (with shareholders supposedly scrutinising private firm managers). It is assumed that by replacing the public enterprise delegation structure (involving the public as principals, the government executive as intermediaries and public enterprise managers as agents) with a private firm delegation structure – by forming a direct link between the principals (the shareholders) and the agent (private firm managers) – the self-seeking behaviour of bureaucrats will be counteracted and the capability of principals to monitor firm performances enhanced.

But the problem of 'agent' accountability to the 'principals' is not by any means eliminated. It persists even in the private firm delegation structure. In so far as private firms are not run by owner-managers, managers may pursue objectives that deviate from owners' objectives.[32] Notwithstanding that, it is also not self-evident that privatisation is the best way to reduce the allegedly harmful inefficiency consequences of public ownership. As Ajit Singh has argued:

> When the shareholder group comprises a large number of individuals, no individual shareholder will have an incentive to collect relevant information and monitor the managers because the individual cannot reap the full benefits from his/her action, because the improved performance is a public good from which every shareholder will benefit without paying for it. In the case of public ownership, there will be a single or at most a few agencies (ministries,

public enterprise agency, public holding companies) who are responsible for the performance of the public enterprises, and therefore there may be less problem of collective action in relation to monitoring activities. In this sense, privatisation can actually worsen public enterprise performance by substituting more effective ministerial monitoring with less effective monitoring through 'shareholder collective action'.[33]

It also appears dubious to attribute the relative effectiveness of the principals in monitoring performance to the number of delegation levels as such. As Ajit Singh maintains:

The distinction between the public and the private enterprises, in terms of the level of delegation is a bogus one. This is because any sizable enterprise, be it public or private, will have more than one layer in the managerial hierarchy. Any large firm is already fraught with the problems of the multiple layers of delegation within the firm. And therefore, it is not clear whether adding one more level of delegation (ministers-managers) to the existing multiplicity of intra-enterprise delegations of authority would make so much difference to the performance of the enterprise.[34]

Indeed, there are many ways by which public enterprise performance can be improved through organisational changes without ownership changes.

On the other hand, the notion of self-seeking bureaucrats forming an essential part of the principal-agent argument is also problematic and may not apply universally. Most importantly, this view is unable to account for the crucial role of public enterprises and bureaucrats in the economies of highly successful NICs, notably South Korea and Taiwan. South Korea has generally had a relatively efficient public sector, including some public enterprises which are among the most efficient in the world. The role and presence of public enterprises in the Taiwanese economy has also been very impressive and prominent by any standards. Rather than make the sweeping conclusion that bureaucrats are invariably self-seeking, it may be more useful to take into account the different political setting and political processes around a bureaucracy in which bureaucrats may not act solely out of self-interest. They can and do act to put the public interest first and regard themselves as guardians of the public interest. Essentially, there may be some sort of consensus that economic development is paramount and it is this that transcends the personal interests of bureaucrats.

Ineffective Disciplinary Mechanisms In Public Enterprises?

It has also been alleged that public enterprises face less pressure to remain as efficient as private firms, as there is no effective disciplinary mechanism to punish bad performance. By contrast, in the case of private firms the disciplinary process is characterised by dissatisfied customers not buying from badly performing firms, which results in falling firm profitability which leads, in turn, to the exit of shareholders. The price of shares will drop due to the selling of shares, which exposes the existing management to the threat of takeover. Management is said to be 'disciplined' into managing the firm efficiently. On the other hand, this disciplinary mechanism attributed to the capital market is not applicable to public enterprise monopolies that do not allow dissatisfied customers an exit option. Moreover, being government bodies, public enterprises are, to a large extent, free from the threat of takeover and bankruptcy. The exclusion of public enterprises from the discipline mechanism of the capital market is said to have contributed to their inefficiency.

This view needs to be qualified. Private ownership *per se* does not necessarily guarantee effective functioning of the exit option. It is commonly asserted that the market mechanism eliminates inefficient or unprofitable firms through the takeover or bankruptcy mechanism, while allowing the more efficient, presumably shareholder-wealth-maximising firms, to prosper. This process, the argument goes, will help develop an economy by ensuring that resources are more efficiently allocated and better utilised. However, Ajit Singh has pointed out that, even in theory, we cannot assume *a priori* that the market for corporate control will work efficiently, due to free-rider problems, transaction costs, and other factors. Crucial to the smooth functioning of this allocative mechanism is the existence of an efficient share pricing process, which ensures greater allocation of new investment resources to well managed, profitable firms by rewarding these firms with higher share prices, thus lowering capital acquiring costs compared to firms with poorer performance. But, as Singh argues, there exists

> a large body of evidence from advanced country stock-markets which indicates that share prices on these markets are generally efficient in the 'information arbitrage' sense: all new information is immediately reflected in share prices. There is, however, far less evidence suggesting that actual prices prevailing on the London or New York stock exchanges are 'efficient' from the point of view of fundamental valuations, i.e. that relative share prices of corporations always reflect their true long-term expected earnings. Many empirical studies have called attention to myopia, fads, and the domination of stock-market prices by short-term considerations. It is the influence of short-termism and speculators on the stock-market that had led Keynes in the General Theory to liken the stock-market to a gambling casino.[35]

Apart from the problem of efficiency pricing, the existence of an efficient takeover mechanism is also put in serious doubt even when share prices are efficient, that is to say they reflect both 'fundamental valuation' and 'information arbitrage' efficiency. Singh observes that:

> twenty years of empirical research suggests that contrary to the folk-lore of capitalism, it is not just the 'inefficient' or 'unprofitable' firms which are eliminated by the takeover mechanism and the 'efficient' and the shareholder-wealth-maximising firms which survive. Empirical studies show that selection for survival in the market for corporate control takes place only to a limited extent on the basis of efficiency or profitability but to a far greater extent on the basis of size. Thus, a large, relative unprofitable company has a much greater chance of being immune from takeover than a much more profitable, but small company. Moreover, on average, profitability of merging firms does not improve after merger. To the extent that the monopoly power of the acquiring firm in the product market increases as a consequence of takeover, the evidence is compatible with reduced efficiency in resource utilisation following mergers. This is hardly the picture of the disciplinary role of the capital market conveyed by the proponents of privatisation.[36]

Ajit Singh also adds that 'instead of disciplining large firms whose managements seek growth for empire building or power motives, the market for corporate control may encourage them to seek a further increase in size precisely in order to avoid being taken over.' It is thus clear that the stock market is not omnipotent, it may not be able to perform well in its disciplinary and allocative tasks, and its activities may actually be damaging to the economy. In fact, the takeover mechanism may actually promote a short-termist outlook on the part of management, impeding the development of long-term investments and the international competitiveness of an economy, to the detriment of its long run growth prospects. The role of stock markets in the developing countries is not unambiguous. Notwithstanding the fact that stock market activities have no significant impact on the growth of aggregate savings in developing countries, the high volatility of share prices and the apparent domination of these markets by speculative activities has seriously impeded the role of stock markets as a guide to the efficient allocation of resources.[37] Hence, the increasing dependence of developing countries on the development of equity markets as part of a strategy for long-term development may be a curse rather than a blessing.

Is Rent-Seeking Necessarily Detrimental to Growth?

Another view that complements the government failure paradigm is the growing literature on rent-seeking behaviour and its generalisation to encompass a wider set of 'directly unproductive profit seeking' (DUP) activities.[38] It sees state intervention as 'directly unproductive' because it diverts resources into unproductive uses as private agents seek to capture rents created by state intervention. Public policies are seen to be largely shaped by the influence of these private agents. Import restrictions, for instance, are presumed to be motivated by the rent-seeking interests of domestic producers, rather than by the more general aim of developing indigenous industries. Rent-seeking is generally seen as a 'waste' from the society's point of view. As Buchanan argues:

> Rent-seeking on the part of potential entrants in a setting where entry is either blocked or can at best reflect one-for-one substitution must generate social waste. Resources devoted to efforts to curry [the authority's] favour might be used to produce valued goods and services elsewhere in the economy, whereas nothing of net value is produced by rent-seeking. In the competitive market, by comparison, resources of potential entrants are shifted directly into the production of the previously monopolised commodity or service, or close substitutes; in this usage, these resources are more productive than they would have been in alternative employments. The unintended results of competitive attempts to capture monopoly rents are 'good' because entry is possible; comparable results of attempts to capture artificially contrived advantageous positions under governmentally enforced monopoly are 'bad' because entry is not possible.[39]

At first sight, the rent-seeking argument appears compelling as an explanation of inefficiency, especially when it takes the form of corruption. Undoubtedly, discussions in the rent-seeking literature have provided important insights with respect to the possible negative consequences of state intervention on the efficiency of an economy. But this only presents half the truth. Firstly, securing access to rent is not necessarily as costly and as wasteful as commonly assumed in the standard rent-seeking literature. Rent-seeking transaction costs (the costs involved in collecting information, influence peddling and bargaining) must be distinguished from the rent itself, which may only be a transfer of wealth and may not involve social costs or wastage. Therefore, 'the mere existence of state-created rents – and therefore, the opportunity of rent-seeking – does not mean that resources will actually be spent on rent-seeking'.[40] Moreover, rent-seeking is not the biggest danger of state intervention. It is often of a once-and-for-all nature, as the rent created may act as an entry barrier that prevents potential entrants from spending extra resources to dislodge the incumbent.

The greater danger is the possibility of the state augmenting and even encouraging inefficient procedures or production methods, with serious long-term efficiency consequences. Though rent-seeking may not have direct efficiency consequences, as it is a pure transfer, it may nevertheless have indirect negative effects on efficiency when it enables less efficient

producers to obtain monopoly rights. This, however, does not justify the
sweeping conclusion that state intervention or state created rents is
a priori harmful. In fact, if the state is able to withdraw the rent whenever
it wishes, rent-seeking may not necessarily be 'directly unproductive'. It
may actually enhance productivity growth – a point not readily
acknowledged in the literature.

> Rent seeking is unambiguously harmful for the society only when it
> can be assumed that the initial institutional creation of an opportunity
> for rent seeking [creation of entry barriers] ensures a net destruction
> of economic value. However, the costs of rent-seeking may well be
> more than offset by the dynamic gains of productivity growth which
> the rent allows, say, by enabling firms to increase R&D expenditure
> – this is precisely the reason why we have, for example, patent
> systems (given the public good nature of technological knowledge)
> and infant industry protection (given the possibility of learning by
> doing). Of course, the theory of rent seeking is correct in arguing
> that free entry is necessary to guarantee the beneficial effects of
> rent, but the theory is far too reluctant to acknowledge that creation
> of monopoly by the state may be beneficial for productivity growth,
> if the state can withdraw the rent whenever necessary.[41]

Amsden has rightly argued that 'instead of viewing rent-seeking as
unbounded, it seems more reasonable to argue that . . . a development
process . . . [can] emerge wherein rent-seeking is present, but not to the
point where it miscarries industrialisation'.[42] As is well known, rent-
seeking activities are by no means alien to the history of politics and
business in South Korea and Taiwan. This has not been an obstacle to,
and may even have facilitated, growth. What needs to be developed is a
more sophisticated theory of government intervention which embraces
this point, rather than *a priori* and *in toto* dismissal of any possibility of a
positive government role in late industrialisation.

It is clear from the foregoing discussion that though there is little
question that government failure has retarded the growth of economic
sectors in many countries, the policy conclusion calling for deregulation
and a minimal government role in the economy does not necessarily
follow. It is often erroneous to attribute government failures to regulations
as such; rather, it should be attributed to the institutional failures which
allow regulation to diminish, rather than enhance economic efficiency.
Besides, the experiences of the NICs have underlined the crucial role of
government in late industrialisation and highlighted distinct areas which
the government may have a definite comparative advantage in
undertaking. This point is well summarised by Chang:

> There can be no presumption that the state will act for the public
> interest . . . However, it is equally inadequate to employ another

sweeping assumption [that calls for deregulation and minimal role of government] . . . What kind of objective function the state would operate with will depend on what kinds of interests can be formed and acted out as a pressure on the state, how resistant the state can be to these demands, what the objectives of the top politicians are, how strongly they control the bureaucracy, how strong hierarchies within the bureaucracy are, how bureaucrats are recruited, what the prevalent ideology within the bureaucracy is and how it is formed.[43]

Indeed, ironically, the success of neo-liberal reform programmes – often introduced at the behest of the World Bank and IMF – generally requires a strong state to mediate the demands of various interest groups 'caused by the imposition of uneven social costs on various segments of the society' as a consequence of the programme. As Moon continues his argument:

Pursuing short-term adjustment and transforming the national economy through neoconservative prescriptions, however, entail formidable political constraints since they inflict substantial social costs and elicit intense political opposition from the affected sectors of society. This is precisely because the reform is usually predicated on a realignment of incentives and benefits among contending social forces. Cutting subsidies, tightly controlling money supply, disciplining labour, readjusting credit allocation, opening up once protected domestic markets and so forth produce a precarious political equation of winners and losers, politicising the entire process of economic reform . . . [Thus] structural adjustment measures which disregard political consequences are bound to fail or at least to be disruptive . . . The Korean experience illustrates that even under tight authoritarian control, structural adjustment efforts invite fierce political opposition and contestation . . . [However], executive dominance, bureaucratic unity and effectiveness, and the relative insulation of economic policy-making and implementation accounted for the Korean success in its [structural adjustment programmes in the early 1980s]. In this sense, state autonomy and strength, if not the authoritarian mode of governance, are a necessary condition for successful structural adjustment. Weak states are very unlikely to initiate and implement coherent, consistent, and effective structural adjustment measures . . . As Latin American experiences explicitly demonstrate, it is for this reason that pluralist democratic regimes are usually unable to implement consistent and coherent neoconservative reforms effectively, resulting in a stop-and-go implementation.[44]

Amsden recognises the same point:

It would be altogether ahistorical to think that getting relative prices 'right' requires any less strength on the state's part than getting them 'wrong'. 'Backward' countries in search of a model to guide them do not present themselves as *tabula rasa*. They have entrenched interest groups that would be hurt if relative prices were 'freed' of distortions. Devaluation hurts firms by raising the cost of imported inputs. Upward adjustments in interest rates hurt investors. Equating of revenues and expenditures in the government budget threatens the livelihood of social welfare recipients, and so on. Whether one attributes the acceleration of growth in Taiwan and Korea to getting relative prices right or wrong, either outcome required strong state management.[45]

IV: A NEW INSTITUTIONALIST ECONOMICS

Hitherto, it has been shown that the neo-liberals have tended to downplay the possible positive role of the state in developing countries. In this section, we look rather briefly at an alternative paradigm, the New Institutionalist Theory of Economics, which looks at the issues of state intervention in a more balanced manner. The Palgrave Economics Dictionary has contrasted neo-classical (including neo-liberal) economics and the New Institutionalist Economics in the following way:

> In contrast with mainstream economics, which maintains that the central economic problems are the allocation of resources, the distribution of income, and the determination of the levels of income, output and prices, institutional economics assert the primacy of the problem of the organisation and control of the economic system, that is, its structure of power. Thus, whereas orthodox economists tend strongly to identify the economy solely with the market, institutional economists argue that the market is itself an institution, comprising a host of subsidiary institutions, and interactive with other institutional complexes in society. The fundamental institutionalist position is that it is not the market but the organisational structure of the larger economy which effectively allocates resources.

Contrary to mainstream thinking, the process of resource allocation is not assumed to be costless, whether it is achieved through market mechanisms or by state intervention: market exchanges or market transactions involve a number of costs, such as search, information, negotiation, contracting, and policing and enforcement costs. These may arise because of an agent's bounded rationality (limits to acquiring and processing information), the opportunistic behaviour of trading partners or asset specificity – which give rise to sunk costs. These are well captured by Chowdhury and Islam:

> [Williamson] identifies a generic class of 'market failure' (i.e. the market will not be efficient in organising transactions) which is conceptually distinct from the familiar ones of externalities and monopoly imperfections. All transactions are characterised by either implicit or explicit contractual arrangements. There are both ex-ante and ex-post costs of negotiating, implementing and enforcing contracts. These transaction costs – which can be particularly acute for complex exchange, such as transfer of technology – stem from bounded rationality and opportunistic behaviour . . . [thus] in the presence of pervasive transaction costs, market failure is common.[46]

Meanwhile, since the state is not omniscient and omnipotent, state intervention is also costly. The problems of bounded rationality and inefficiencies resulting from 'opportunistic' behaviour are present, constituting the costs of government intervention. These market exchange and governing costs are generally characterised as transaction costs. And if transaction costs are high, market failure or government failure – generally characterised as institutional failure – may result. The crucial question is how each institution in an economy can be exploited to best advantage, so that exchange does not break down, and resources can be effectively allocated through the right institutional mix. Hence, the question of whether an imperfect market is superior to an imperfect government is wrongly framed, and the strong faith placed on a freely functioning market in promoting growth – with almost total denial of a positive role for government – seems misplaced. As Mustapha Nabli sees it:

> It has long been recognised that traditional neoclassical economics, by taking institutions as given or failing to recognise their relevance for the analysis of economic problems, has been unable to provide satisfactory explanations for a wide range of conditions commonly found in LDCs. For example, neither general references to market imperfections and distortions nor detailed analyses of their welfare consequences help explain either the pervasiveness of these imperfections and distortions or the considerable difficulties in removing them . . . [Further] in such analyses, the institutional framework has almost invariably been taken as given, and in many cases, has even been altogether omitted. The consequence of taking the institutional framework as given has [ignored and downplayed the role of institutional innovation in development], and it is especially unrealistic and limiting in the context of economic development, a process whereby institutions generally undergo substantial change.[47]

'The real question is whether the state can achieve the same allocative efficiency at a lower cost than the market, and not whether state intervention is costly *per se*'.[48] In fact, there need not be antagonism between the state and the market in promoting development; both can be complementary. The market need not be the only viable coordination mechanism, while the state – along with the market and other economic institutions – can be an important means of coordination. In fact, it may be more promising to reconceptualise the question of development from a different perspective:

> Can we improve our understanding of development by understanding how efficient economic organisations are to different countries? Do we have to think entirely in terms of increasing the resources available to a country, through loans, gifts, or other means, in order for a country to develop? Or can we get equal or better results by analysing the organisations involved, suggesting means for change, and changing the institutional environment under which such organisations operate? [And] to what extent can growth be retarded by the inability to innovate institutionally.[49]

Indeed, reliance on the market as the only viable agent for promoting growth seems inadequate. In her endeavour to provide a theory of government intervention for late industrialisation, Amsden has argued that the inability of poorer countries to industrialise is due to the workings and not the failure of the market.

> [A]s late industrialisers must grow exclusively by borrowing technology [and] . . . [d]enied a competitive advantage from new products and processes, they initially have to rely only on their low wages to wrest market shares . . . Low wages, however, are an inadequate basis of industrialisation . . . State intervention is necessary even in the most plausible cases of comparative advantage, because the chief asset of backwardness – low wages – is counterbalanced by heavy liabilities . . . the level of international competition, the technology gap, the investment barriers and savings deficiencies, are all so problematic, that without government intervention, little ever gets done to address these hurdles . . . Thus, late industrialisation should not be conceived as a consequence of international wage differential or a movement up the ladder of comparative advantage but has occurred largely as a direct consequence of actions taken by underdeveloped countries themselves.[50]

'Backwardness' may seriously impede a market driven growth process. In such economies, the mere workings of the market are inadequate for achieving late industrialisation. Indeed, one of Amsden's central theses is the proposition that the mode by which late industrialisation occurs (through learning by borrowing, adapting and improving upon foreign designs) is different from industrialisation in the eighteenth century, which occurred on the basis of invention, and that of the nineteenth century, which occurred on the basis of innovation.

> The firms of the late industrialisers then have to compete with those established firms that can introduce new technologies fast enough to capture 'technology rents' and thereby earn higher profits. This does, of course, allow the late industrialisers to acquire, or 'borrow', the more codified elements of a given technology wihout having to develop them for itself. But there is generally a great gap between buying or stealing the codified elements and mastering the technology in production. The lower labor costs of the late industrialisers offer another partial advantage in such competition. But since its labor force is much less skilled, the lower labor costs may not compensate for differences in productivity. Late industrialisers all tend to construct a similar set of institutions to respond to the handicaps and advantages of lateness. In particular, they tend to develop entrepreneurial and diversified business groups.[51]

A strong interventionist state is a prerequisite for late industrialising countries to succeed. Amsden argues that in the absence of novel technology the state needs to intervene and deliberately distort prices to stimulate investment and trade – in particular, the government needs to subsidise and discipline business.

> The main problem of late industrialisers is that they cannot compete at market-determined prices because their productivity is so low . . . productivity gaps between developed and underdeveloped countries widened in the 20th century, overpowering the competitive advantage of cheap labor . . . one reason for the lengthy delay in catching up – even in industries in which technology can be bought on competitive terms and in which labor costs are a sizeable share of total costs – relates to the cat-and-mouse quality of competition, a dynamic which standard price theory largely ignores. Foreign competitors may be expected to introduce a stream of new innovations in productivity and quality to retaliate for their loss of market share, and it takes time for late industrialisers to build a team of engineers and a workforce with the capabilities to keep abreast of these advances . . . This proposition is lent empirical support by the industrialisation problems of Japan versus Lancashire in the early 1900s; or the difficulties which South Korea and Taiwan faced in competing against Japan beginning in the 1960s; or the troubles China encountered vis-a-vis Japan in the 1930s, and so forth. Devoid of major innovation, [late industrialisation] is predicated on

borrowing technology and then improving it incrementally, [thus] leading enterprises in twentieth century industrialisation must be subsidised . . . During what may be lengthy periods of subsidisation to arrive at productivity levels that are cost-competitive, market forces cannot be relied upon to discipline business to act efficiently – i.e. to invest heavily in adapting foreign technology, and then to invest further in incremental improvements in quality and productivity in order to compete against foreign imports or capture export markets. [They] do not have the incentive to compete to the extent of becoming as efficient as the firm at the world technological frontier.[52]

Meanwhile, the crucial role of the state in shaping and transforming class structure in a society is often ignored in the neo-classical and neo-liberal traditions – in spite of the fact that the pattern of ownership of productive assets often has profound impacts on production and growth. As Hamilton shows in his comparative study of the four Asian NICs, the state's active incorporation of an industrial workforce was central to the process of industrialisation.[53] Hence, 'getting the prices right' is, at best, necessary – in the sense of augmenting market competition and enhancing productivity – but certainly not sufficient in stimulating the industrialisation characterising the rapid growth of South Korea and Taiwan. Based on transaction economics, Lee and Lee argue that:

> '[I]nternal implementation' by a quasi-internal organisation could be more effective than 'market implementation' in achieving necessary developmental goals. Non-market hierarchical allocation helps to resolve the problems of imperfect markets and policy implementation because such a network structure allows for the specialisation of decision making, economises on communication costs, and reduces uncertainty by co-ordinating the decisions of interdependent units in adapting to unforeseen contingencies . . . [in fact] intervention in South Korea and Taiwan did not ignore the markets . . . it was 'market-augmenting' in the sense that it reduced the uncertainties and risks related to business, generated and disseminated information about opportunities, and installed expansion psychology in the people. This was opposed to 'market-suppressing' planning which entails the increasing fragmentation of the market or the proliferation of rent-seeking opportunities.[54]

Thus, according to the transactions cost branch of the New Institutional Economics, it is the institutional arrangements (which cover a broader institutional setting than is recognised by the neo-classicals) that minimise the cost of transactions, and thus constitute the key to the performance of various economies. As pointed out by Mustapha Nabli, by affecting transaction costs and coordination possibilities, institutions can have the effect of either facilitating or retarding economic growth. The choice of appropriate political institutions, rules and policies enhances economic growth. Moreover, by affecting resource mobililty and the incentives for innovation and accumulation, institutions may induce or hinder economic efficiency in the allocation of resources and growth.[55]

V: A LIBERAL-NEUTRAL TRADE REGIME?

Having considered the theoretical discussion of government growth, we now turn to evidence from the East Asian NICs, often invoked by neo-liberals as examples *par excellence* of free market economies. Wade has distinguished between free market and simulated market versions of the neo-classical account of East Asian success.[56] According to the free market components, East Asian economies have done better than other countries because the East Asian states practised a 'hands-off' *laissez-faire* policy to ensure undistorted and therefore optimal workings of market forces. On the other hand, it contends, other countries have not been successful in making their way up the development ladder – what they would otherwise have achieved in the 'normal' course of events – due to excessive state intervention, especially in foreign trade. This view is exemplified by Edward Chen, Milton and Rose Friedman, John Fei and David Aikman, among others. Some neo-classical economists, however, have not completely ruled out a role for governments in East Asia; they concede that the governments have done more than just liberalise markets and minimise distortions. In their view, the governments have played a positive role in offsetting distortions caused by government-induced policies (for example, import controls) and earlier government failure to change distortion-inducing institutions directly (for example, segmented financial markets). This view, which attributes a greater role to government in simulating the market, is called the simulated free market theory by Wade and exemplified by Jagdish Bagwati, Frederick Berger and Gary Saxonhouse, among others.

The simulated free market theory differs from free market theory by invoking the distinction between a free trade regime and a neutral trade regime. The former is identified with a liberal trade regime, one with no or few impediments to imports; the latter, however, should not be equated with the absence of government intervention, because it refers to a structure where a bias against imports (for example, due to protection) is neutralised by a bias favouring exports (for example, by export subsidies), and trade policies do not selectively discriminate among industries except as necessary to overcome market failure. In essence, both free market and simulated market theories claim that smoothly functioning markets –

achieving efficient resources allocation – have been a prerequisite for growth, and attribute the superior performance of East Asian economies to the efficient functioning of their markets compared to other developing countries.

Robert Wade has contended that while South Korea and Taiwan have met many neo-classical conditions unusually well, the governments' role has also been much more prominent than suggested by either free market or simulated market theory, a fact completely overlooked in the mainstream literature. Over the past decade or so, another stream of literature has emphasised the directive role of the state in East Asia. Research by Amsden, Deyo, Dornbusch and Park, Hamilton, and many others has underlined the importance of state intervention in promoting growth in the NICs.[57] This approach

> focuses upon the importance of the class base and the relative autonomy of the state, its administrative capacity, its ability to make long-run strategic decisions, and the role of intermediate levels of state intervention in the formulation and execution of a selective industrial policy.[58]

Wade's governed market theory argues that the superiority of East Asian economic performance is due, in large measure, to the effectiveness of industrial policy in developing or retrenching various industries in a national economy in order to maintain global competitiveness. Specifically, it is due

> to a combination of (1) very high levels of productive investment, making for fast transfer of newer techniques into actual production; (2) more investment in certain key industries than would have occurred in the absence of government intervention; and (3) exposure of many industries to international competition, in foreign markets, if not at home. They have managed to achieve this because of a set of government economic policies. Using incentives, controls and mechanisms to spread risk, these policies enabled the government to guide – or govern – market processes of resource allocation so as to produce different production and investment outcomes than would have occurred with either free market or simulated free market policies.[59]

In other words, the government has led, and not followed, the market. The government market theory also says that

> government policies deliberately got some prices 'wrong' so as to change the signals to which decentralized market agents responded, and also used non-price means to alter the behaviour of market agents. Various trade incentives and control instruments coupled

with mechanisms to spread risk have allowed the governments to guide the market processes of resource allocation, producing different investment and production outcomes than would have occurred with either free or simulated market policies.[60]

In the remaining sections, we will look more closely at the role of state in promoting development in some Northeast Asian economies, and, more specifically, examine the extent to which free market and simulated market conditions have been present over time, and to what extent they have been important in accounting for late industrialisation in the region.

VI: POROUS STATE INTERVENTION IN NORTHEAST ASIA?

Before we turn our attention to the role of industrial policy in promoting development, it is worthwhile to look at Bhagwati's interpretation of government intervention in East Asia. Unlike his neo-liberal counterparts, he explicitly recognises that there has been considerable government intervention in the East Asian economies.

> For those who seek in the experiences of [the NICs economies] an endorsement of free trade in the context of passive government, these facts present obvious difficulties . . . These countries have highly energetic and involved governments . . . The key question is not whether there is governmental action in the Far Eastern economies, but rather how these successful economies have managed their intervention and their strategic decision making better than the unsuccessful economies.[61]

But, according to Bhagwati, the positive role of government is only limited to increasing producers' confidence in the government's commitment to export-led growth, which in turn induces firms to undertake costly investments and programmes as part of a national export-promotion strategy. He argues that the superior economic performance of the NICs is largely attributable to governments which issue 'prescriptions' identifying 'dos', rather than 'proscriptions' identifying 'don'ts'. Such intervention is said to explain the rapid growth of the NICs as 'a proscriptive government will tend to stifle initiative, whereas a prescriptive government will tend to leave open areas where initiative can be exercised'.[62]

However, the distinction between a prescriptive and proscriptive government is problematic and ambiguous. When a government prescribes something, it is indirectly – and sometimes directly – proscribing something else (with the converse also true). There seems to be a problem of sophistry in Bhagwati's distinction. It does not say anything meaningful about the nature of government intervention by characterising it as 'prescriptive' or 'proscriptive'. At another level, it is also unclear why

'although a prescriptive government may prescribe as badly as a proscriptive government proscribes, a proscriptive government will tend to
stifle initiatives, whereas a prescriptive government will tend to leave
open areas where initiative can be exercised'.[63] Presumably, a proscriptive
government may proscribe little and leave considerable room for initiative.
Conversely, a prescriptive government may stifle initiative 'since it can
make private enterprises do so many things against their will that they are
left with little resources to do what they want, even if these activities
are not explicitly forbidden'.[64] More importantly, however, Bhagwati's
analysis has largely failed to capture the dynamics of government intervention in East Asia. Though the South Korean state is characterised by
Bhagwati as a 'prescriptive' state, government prescriptions there were
certainly 'stifling' in many ways while 'proscriptive' intervention by the
state has not been so minimal as to warrant the label 'prescriptive' without
serious qualifications.

VII: INDUSTRIAL POLICY

Industrial policy, as one important area of state intervention, has received
considerable attention with the rise and growing importance of East
Asian economies. Chang has defined industrial policy

> as a policy aimed to affect particular industries (and firms and their
> components) to achieve the outcomes which are perceived by the
> state to be efficient for the economy as a whole. This definition is
> closer to what is usually called 'selective industrial policy' . . . more
> concretely, it means the state selectively monitoring entry, estab-
> lishing mechanism to make possible more *ex ante* coordination than
> is possible through market mechanism alone and for governmental
> regulation or overview to constrain or supplement profit incentives.[65]

Johnson has similarly characterised industrial policy in South Korea and
Taiwan as 'the infusion of co-ordinated goal oriented strategic thinking
into public economic policy [which] seeks to leverage upward the productivity and competitiveness of the whole economy and of particular
industries'.[66]

Static Dimensions of Industrial Policy

In the model of perfect competition, *ex ante* coordination is superfluous
because the market is assumed to be a coordination device *par excellence*.
As it is assumed that each firm's output is infinitesimally small (or
negligible), independent actions by a single firm are unable to change the
aggregate outcome, and the workings of the market will ensure that a
societally optimal output will be produced most efficiently. Hence, *ex
ante* coordination is redundant, as, 'when individuals are negligible, there

is no interdependence among individual agents and hence no need to coordinate their activities', although, to ensure total absence of interdependence, production technology has to be assumed to be characterised by decreasing returns to scale.[67] However, even under the standard assumption of constant returns to scale (CRS) – not to mention the problematic case of increasing returns to scale – pure competition may not clear the market.

> When CRS technology prevails in a large number of settings, *ex ante*, firms may behave as if the demand curve is horizontal, but *ex post*, there is no guarantee that the market will clear, since an individual firm, not being bound by production technology, can produce as much as it wants. In other words, there is no way to determine the number of the firms and their respective outputs in an industry characterised by a CRS production technology, as is recognised even by standard neo-classical texts. Therefore, even with CRS technology there may be so few firms in a market as to give rise to interdependence and consequently to the need for *ex ante* coordination.[68]

Moreover, as Williamson states,

> it does not suffice to demonstrate that a condition of large members competition obtains at the outset. It is also necessary to examine whether this continues or if, by reason of transaction specific investments and incomplete contracting, a condition of bilateral trading evolves thereafter.[69]

Conceivably, the problem of coordination may not have existed if firms are assumed to possess foreknowledge of other firms' actions, thus allowing them to adjust their level of output. However, this assumption is fallacious. As Hayek notes:

> The statement that, if people know everything, they are in equilibrium, is true simply because that is how we define equilibrium . . . [and] a state of affairs which economic theory curiously calls 'perfect competition', i.e. a situation in which all the facts are supposed to be known 'leaves' no room whatever for the activity called competition.[70]

In fact, if every firm has perfect knowledge, any coordination mechanism will be redundant, including the price system. Hence, as Chang argues: '. . . equilibrium in the perfect competition model is attained only because the coordination problem is assumed away from the beginning!'[71] On the other hand, in the model of oligopoly, the problem of coordination arising from market indetermination is explicitly recognised by neo-classical orthodoxy. However, their solutions are inadequate and unsatisfactory. To quote Chang again:

Models of oligopoly in the Neoclassical tradition recognise the coordination problem arising from the indeterminacy of the market outcome in a small number of settings. However, their solutions to the coordination problem are not entirely satisfactory. The usual solution to the problem is to employ the concept of the mixed (randomised) strategy. However, a mixed strategy does not guarantee an optimal solution except in the probabilistic sense that, if the situation occurred an infinite number of times, randomising one's actions would yield the highest average payoff. When the situation is not recurrent, employing the concept of probability is less than meaningful, and it is therefore dubious to describe the mixed strategy equilibrium as optimal. For example, how can firm A's strategy regarding its investment in production capacity for 4 Mb memory chip be 'randomised' in any meaningful sense, when, given the speed of technical progress, it is clear that the next round of investment will be in 16Mb memory chip capacity?

One way of avoiding the difficulty of employing probabilistic behaviour by individual agents in non-recurrent situations is to interpret the mixed strategy as an 'evolutionarily stable strategy' (ESS) whereby individual agents do not randomise their actions but there are sufficient different types of agents in the population for the aggregate outcome to be the same as when individual agents randomise . . . However, even in the biological world, where the concept originated, the ESS equilibrium holds only approximately, because [genetic] heterogeneity and changing conditions must mean that often populations are not perched at adaptive peaks. Even when the conditions are constant, selection becomes progressively weaker towards the peak of a continuous fitness function; infinite time and infinite populations would be needed to achieve the peak itself . . . And the intuitive meaning of ESS becomes even less clear in many industrial markets where the 'condition' changes so rapidly that the selection mechanism does not have the time to work to the full extent and where the agents (being humans) learn and change not only their 'genes' (behavioural characteristics), but also the selection mechanism (the environment) and consequently the ESS itself.[72]

If the market is deficient in solving coordination problems then there is a case for non-market *ex ante* coordination. However, it may be counter-argued that the disciplinary mechanism of the market will ensure an optimal number of firms in the industry, thus making any *ex ante* co-ordination unnecessary; if more than an optimal number of firms entered the industry (for example in industries with increasing returns to scale), competitive forces will force the exit (through bankruptcy) of inefficient firms, thereby ensuring an optimal outcome. This notion is based on the questionable assumption that resources are perfectly mobile and can be instantaneously and costlessly shifted to other activities. In practice,

> assets are often 'specific' to the investments and therefore cannot be redeployed without a loss of value . . . In a world with asset specificity, *ex post* coordination through the market can be wasteful . . . because coordination failure which involves specific assets means a net reduction in the amount of resources available to the economy.[73]

Industrial Policy As A Device of Coordination

From a static perspective, industrial policy can help to play a complementary role (to the market) in the area of coordination. As we have seen, coordination is constantly a problem not fully resolved by the market mechanism. Specifically, it can be used to avoid the problems of under- or over-investment in certain industries by organising recession cartels to cushion the effect of unforeseen fluctuations in demand and to assist in the adjustment process of capacity scrapping and the inevitable exit of certain firms in declining industries. Leaving those adjustments to market forces may be costly as it may lead to a protracted price war which may make everyone worse off than would be the case with timely exit. One of the fundamental features characterising a modern industrial economy is the large fixed investments in production technology often entailing significant scale economies. Thus, scale economies necessitate the existence of only a few firms in an industry. And out of fear of being outcompeted by the more efficient firms, other firms in the industry will have the incentive to adopt the same (or more efficient) technology. Under such circumstances, strategic interdependence in firms' decision making becomes important and provides a case for state intervention. Industrial policy can be used as a device for coordination to avoid problems of under- or over-investment in certain industries under particular economic circumstances. Under adverse economic conditions, firms in this industry are likely to engage in price wars (selling at losses to undercut competitors) to secure greater market shares so as to cover their heavy fixed costs. Such excessive competition can cause 'fratricidal' warfare, high bankruptcy rates, large layoffs and industrial disorder. The government can step in and organise anti-recession cartels (as in Japan and South Korea) to limit supply, restrain price competition, and agree on investment levels.

However, in orthodox thinking, cartel arrangements are economic vices, seen as creating deadweight losses, resulting in allocative inefficiencies. If the possible benefits of cartels outweigh the deadweight losses, cartels may nevertheless be a feasible and desirable option. Firstly, if bankruptcy involved social waste due to the specificity of assets, a recession cartel could alleviate the problem. Secondly, if there is no social waste due to bankruptcy, a price war could induce allocative inefficiency in the long run as firms surviving the price war will eventually extract more monopoly profits after recovery. Finally, the price war may have long-lasting negative consequences 'on long term productivity growth as firms reduce their investment level to compensate for the losses incurred in the price war'.[74]

On the other hand, problems of over- or under-investment in a new industry (or an expanding industry) with scale economies can be attenuated by the use of industrial policy. Potential entrants may underestimate the number of entrants to the industry, resulting in excessive (or insufficient) investment in the industry producing a suboptimal output. According to Chang:

> Since under- and over-investments are essentially problems of strategic uncertainty (each potential entrant not knowing the intentions of the others), the state can intervene in this industry to assure optimal entry by guaranteeing potential entrants that there will not be more than optimal entry. It can do this through arbitrating private bargainings among potential entrants, but also by superceding private dealings and thus reducing transaction costs involved in such bargainings. Licensing entry and regulating capacity expansion are the most common forms of state-imposed investment coordination .[75]

If the industry is structurally depressed (that is, experiencing long-term demand downturn), unlikely ever to regain competitiveness (just as aluminium, petrochemicals, paper and pulp, petroleum refining and some parts of the steel industry have run into trouble) and if there is a specific asset involved, there is a case for a government-augmented orderly exit or capacity scrapping programme. A contrary arrangement could provoke a protracted price war that leaves everyone worse off than they would have been with timely exits (on the assumption that all the firms are on more or less equal footing).

Dynamic Dimensions of Industrial Policy

Industrial policy is concerned with creating dynamic comparative advantage, as opposed to the static or classical notion of comparative advantage which underlines geographical or natural endowment differences to produce a global division of labour. In the words of Johnson,

> industrial targeting, or dynamic anticipation of the economically efficient allocation of resources for the future becomes an important tool for the East Asian economies. The government explicitly identifies and promotes certain industries and technologies that they anticipate will be important for the competitiveness and well-being of the economy in the future.[76]

At a more basic level, the promotional role of industrial policy is based on the concept of the 'product cycle'. As Chang observes:

> In the infant stage of an industry where experimentation is necessary to generate new knowledge, industrial policy should encourage it. More aggressive experimentation and learning can be encouraged by providing firms with a more stable environment (through, say, patent system, subsidies, tariffs, or other types of entry barriers) . . . it has an important coordinating role to play at this stage. Introducing national product, and if necessary, process standards, coordinating competing investment decisions to prevent under-investment and overinvestment, and ensuring that complementary investments are made will all be useful at this stage . . . As the market 'matures', most technical knowledges become codified and easily transmittable. As a few technologies emerge as the 'best practice' ones, they are adopted across the industry, as firms learn from the experiences of others, [the involvement of the government will fall off significantly]. As an industry enters its senile stage, production shrinks, labour is shed, and capacity is scrapped. The material and human resources employed in an industry may be highly specific to that industry so that their deployment may be extremely difficult . . . The role of industrial policy in this phase will be to encourage private negotiation regarding exit and capacity scrapping between the relevant agents . . . retraining and relocation programmes organised by the state will also greatly assist the process of negotiation, by reducing the would-be displaced workers' resistance to the firm's decision to exit or scrap the capacity.[77]

However, one common objection to the use of industrial policy for dynamically promoting certain strategic industries is the problem of information. It is said that the state lacks the necessary information to 'pick the winners' (sunrise industries) and is hence incapable of deciding the future industrial structure of the economy. Hence, the argument goes, the state should support a generalised industrial policy (supporting certain types of activities such as investment and R&D) rather than adhering to a selective industrial policy targeting particular industries. Admittedly, as correctly perceived by the opponents of industrial policy, there is indeed a risk of policy failure due to lack of information. But the policy conclusion calling for a generalised industrial policy may not be tenable and justified. As Chang notes:

> The informational problem, we agree, is often a very serious one . . . however, we would argue that the informational problem can be exaggerated and that it is solvable . . . First of all, it is simply not true that private firms operate on the basis of perfect knowledge

while bureaucrats know nothing about business. Private firms themselves often operate on the basis of 'informed guesses' or 'animal
spirits' when they make major investment decisions, especially in
new industries. In addition, large private firms, and not just the state,
suffer from informational problems in controlling their divisions
and subsidiaries . . . [It] is inadequate to argue that the state should
not attempt to plan the future of the national economy because of
insufficient information when firms can and do plan their own future
despite – or rather, precisely because of – insufficient information.

   And when the state maintains an efficient information network of
its own, as in the case of Korea, the informational gap between the
private sector and the state may be virtually non-existent. The
Korean state has kept very close track of priority industries through
the obligatory reporting system. And, in some respects, the state
may often be better informed than the private sector, as exemplified
by the important role played by the information collected by
Korean state agencies, including the diplomatic service, and, more
importantly, KOTRA (Korean Trade Promotion Corporation), in
the penetration of new export markets by Korean firms . . . Further,
the difficulties of identifying 'sunrise' industries is not as great as
often made out by opponents of industrial policy, except perhaps on
the very frontier of technological development. There usually exists
a widespread consensus as to which industries are 'sunrise' industries.
For example, we all know that, say, automobile and microelectronics
industries are going to be important in the conceivable future.
Especially in 'catching up' situations, it is fairly easy to identify
which sectors to favour and what kind of support is required for
success. The fact that the Korean economic bureaucracy has been
traditionally manned by lawyers (at least until the 1970s) also
suggests that 'expert' knowledge may not be necessary for solving
the informational problem.[78]

   Indeed, the success of industrial policy in Japan, South Korea and
Taiwan have provided convincing empirical support for the validity of
industrial policy as a legitimate tool in promoting industrial development
in late industrialising countries. In these countries, the market is not
viewed as an end that is sufficient in itself. Instead, the state needs to play
an active role in 'harnessing, directing, and spurring' the market to
achieve desirable transformation of industrial structure for the development of a vigorous, dynamic and competitive economy.[79] In particular,
the government has been involved in establishing priority sectors; mobilising resources to hasten their development; protecting infant industries;
allocating foreign exchange credit; regulating technological flows; controlling direct foreign investment; organising rationalisation and recession

cartels; pacifying and co-opting labour; ensuring the effective flow of financial resources to designated priority sectors. It is sufficient here to cite MITI's industrial policy in Japan's economy. Okimoto analyses its role by means of a product life cycle intervention pattern:

> MITI intervention tends to follow a curvilinear trajectory; i.e. extensive involvement during the early stages of an industry's life cycle when market demand is still small, falling off significantly as the industry reaches full maturity and demand reaches its peak, and rising again as industry loses comparative advantage and faces the problems of senescence – saturated markets, the loss of market share, and excess capacity . . .[80]

In Japan, the sunrise industries of data processing, computer software, biotechnology, space, ocean development and nuclear energy and the sunset industries of iron and steel, textiles and chemicals, being at early and later stages of development respectively, have received the highest levels of government support. The support falls off significantly in industries which have reached maturity, respectively integrated circuits, automobiles, industrial machines and consumer electronics.

Evidently, industrial policy is a highly relevant and important tool for manoeuvre in late industrialisation, but, needless to say, it is not without costs in rent-seeking and policy failure. But the experience of the East Asian countries has shown that the benefits have generally outweighed the costs, and that industrial policy has not been used to supplant the market, but to complement it. Most importantly, it has helped to socialise risk. As Chang argues:

> If the risks involved in these situations have to be solely borne by the individuals, necessary changes may not come about. The socialisation of risk through state intervention is a means of promoting changes which involve interdependence . . . and institutional arrangements, which by internalising benefits and externalising costs of private investment allow experimentation and risk-taking beyond a scale whose risk can personally be borne out by the experimenter, have played an important role.[81]

VIII: CONCLUSION

Undoubtedly, the experiences of the East Asian economies of South Korea and Taiwan have tremendous relevance for late industrialisation in developing countries, lessons not to be found in World Bank structural adjustment programmes. Chang has correctly pointed out that development strategy is a complex set of interrelated policies, and should not be misconceived as a simple dichotomy between 'outward looking' (EOI) strategies and 'inward looking' (ISI) strategies – with the commonplace argument that export orientation is more conducive to rapid overall growth than import substituting industrialisation. In fact, as pointed out by Manuel R. Agosin,

> the inconclusive nature of the evidence advanced in the recent literature . . . suggests that the extent to which growth is correlated positively to outward orientation will vary from country to country. There is no reason to expect on *a priori* grounds that import substitution must be in all cases an inferior option.[82]

Besides, development strategy is multidimensional; it is concerned with the 'establishment of long term targets for growth, structural change' and enhancing productivity and competitiveness in the economy, rather than the static conception of an export-led strategy relying on exports of labour-intensive products for growth.[83] Moreover, there may be no unique optimum degree of openness which applies to all countries. A country may be open in certain areas (for example trade), but closed in others (for example capital and financial markets). As Chakravarty and Singh's analysis suggests, a number of factors may affect the desirable degree of openness: the world situation, the past history of the economy, its state of development, and so on.[84] Wrong timing and sequencing in 'opening' an economy can have disastrous results. Indeed, both paths may not be mutually exclusive alternatives. They can be complementary and interactive, as suggested by the experiences of Japan, South Korea and Taiwan.

The success of industrial policy in the East Asian economies suggests that the state in developing countries can indeed play a positive and crucial role in late industrialisation. The economic performances of the East Asian late industrialising countries owe much to government initiative and intervention, but governments in most LDCs have also played significant, if not major, roles in promoting development. But the difference between what has happened in East Asia and experiences elsewhere does not lie in the discovery of industrial policy instruments not known elsewhere. Many other nations have, at one time or another, tried most of the policy tools used in East Asia. What differentiates their efforts, above all, is a consistent and coordinated attentiveness to the problems and opportunities of particular industries, in the context of a long-term perspective of the economy's evolution, and a state which is 'hard' enough not only to have significant effects on the economy, but also to control the direction of the effects, which is more demanding.

While it is evident that industrial policy has been critical to the success of the NICs, the crucial question is why the governments of Taiwan and South Korea were apparently able to reap the potential benefits of industrial policy, when many other governments could not. It is not simply true, as claimed by Balassa, that the role of the state 'apart from the promotion of ship building and steel in Korea and of a few strategic industries in Taiwan . . . has been to create a modern infrastructure, to provide a stable incentive system, and to ensure that government bureaucracy will help rather than hinder exports', while in Latin American countries, 'there are pervasive controls of investment, prices, and imports, and decisions are generally made on a case by case basis, thereby creating uncertainty for business decisions'.[85] The policy measures used in South Korea and Taiwan are not radically different from those used in Latin America and other developing countries. As Pack and Westphal argue:

> Incentives policies having a strong industry-bias together with credit rationing, import quotas, licensing controls and many other of the overt instruments of selective intervention that have been widely castigated [and applied unsuccessfully elsewhere] by the neoclassicals have been used with apparently very successful results by [the East Asian] countries . . . The differences are to be found instead in different ways of using the same policy instruments – for example, in the scope of their application, in whether they are used promotionally or restrictively.[86]

The answers seem to rest on three points.[87] Firstly, the central economic bureaucrats of East Asian countries seem to have realised that mere protection has not been sufficient to generate rapid growth. They sought to couple protection with competition, to ensure that the lethargy-inducing effects of protection were outweighed by the efficiency-inducing policies. Secondly, interventions have been selective, and the criteria of selection have to do with future competitiveness. This serves to differentiate East Asian intervention from much of Latin American and Indian intervention, where the assumption has tended to be that trade controls, coupled with unselective support of all domestic market oriented industrial investment, would be sufficient to promote the right kind of industrialisation. Thirdly, even more important than the market-augmenting method of intervention, has been the willingness and ability of the state to discipline capital. Incentives have not been allocated as give-aways, but rather in exchange for meeting specific concrete performance standards, with respect to output, exports, product quality, investments in training and, more recently, R&D. To be sure, the role of government in the Northeast Asian late industrialising economies is of interest to all LDCs making their way up the development ladder. However, direct emulation of these experiences may not be feasible and their experiences not easily transferable from one context to another, as their development strategies have been born out of particular historical, social and political circumstances. But their experience may nevertheless be illuminating, serving to refute the vulgar neo-liberal contentions and helping to point the way in which the role of state in developing countries can be more concretely defined and industrial policy – in its various forms and degrees – can be effectively employed – depending on the size, structure and stage of development of the different economies and the nature of their states and societies.

NOTES

1. J. Tobin, 'One or Two Cheers for the Invisible Hand', in S. Rhee and R.P. Chang (eds.), *Pacific-Basin Capital Market Research* (Holland, 1990). Unless otherwise specified, economic neo-liberalism is a reference to the works of Balassa, Bauer, Krueger, Lal, and Little.
2. D. Lal, *The Poverty of Development Economics* (London, 1983).
3. Ibid., pp.27–8; I.M.D. Little, 'An Economic Reconnaissance', in W. Galenson (ed.), *Economic Growth and Structural Change in Taiwan: The Postwar Experiences of the Republic of China* (Ithaca, 1979), pp.474, 480; E. Chen, *Hyper-Growth in Asian Economies: A Comparative Study of Hong Kong, Japan, Korea, Singapore and Taiwan* (London, 1979).
4. A. Amsden, 'A Theory of Government Intervention in Late-Industrialisation', Working Paper, New School for Social Research, No.27 (New York), pp.14–15.
5. See quote in R. Wade, 'East Asia Economic Success: Conflicting Perspectives, Partial Insights, Shaky Evidence', *World Politics*, Vol.44 (1992).
6. A. Krueger, 'Trade Policy as an Input to Development', *American Economic Review*, Vol.70 (1980).
7. See D. Rodrik, 'How Should Structural Adjustment Programs be Designed?', *World Development*, Vol.18 (1990).
8. See Rodrik, 'How Should . . .'.
9. H. Stein, 'Deindustrialisation Adjustment, the World Bank and the IMF in Africa', *World Development*, Vol.20 (1992).
10. See C.I. Bradford, 'Trade and Structural Change: NICs and Next Tier NICs as Transitional Economies', *World Development*, Vol.15 (1987).
11. G. Rodan, *The Political Economy of Singapore's Industrialisation: National State and International Capital* (London, 1989), p.6.
12. D. Evans and P. Alizadeh, 'Trade, Industrialisation and the Invisible Hand', *The Journal of Development Studies*, Vol.21 (1984).
13. C. Edwards, *The Fragmented World: Competing Perspectives on Trade, Money and Crises* (New York, 1985), pp.123–34.
14. Amsden, 'Theory of Government Intervention', pp.14–15.
15. Evans and Alizadeh, 'Trade, Industrialisation . . .'
16. I. Little, T. Scitovsky and M. Scott, *Industry and Trade in Some Development Countries: A Comparative Study* (New York, 1970); B. Balassa, 'Industrial Policies in Taiwan and Korea', *Weltwirtschaftliches Archiv*, Vol.106 (1971).
17. World Bank, *World Development Report* (Washington DC, 1981 and 1987).
18. B. Balassa, 'The Lessons of East Asian Development: An Overview', *Economic Development and Cultural Change*, Vol.36 (1988).
19. Evans and Alizadeh, 'Trade, Industrialisation . . .'.
20. R. Jenkins, 'Reinterpreting Brazil and South Korea', in T. Hewitt, H. Johnson and D. Wield (eds.), *Industrialisation and Development* (Oxford, 1992).
21. C. Colclough, 'Structuralism versus Neoliberalism: An Introduction', in C. Colclough and J. Manor (eds.), *States or Markets? Neoliberalism and the Development Policy Debate* (Oxford, 1991), p.10.
22. J. Toye, *Dilemmas of Development* (Oxford, 1987).
23. R. Wade, *Governing the Market: Economic Theory and the Role of Government in East Asian Industrialisation* (Princton, 1990).
24. D. Evans, 'Visible and Invisible Hands in Trade Policy Reform', in Colclough and Manor, 'States or Markets?', p.49.
25. Lal, 'Poverty of Development Economics'.

26. Ibid.
27. Evans, 'Visible and Invisible Hands', p.56.
28. A. Krueger, 'Government Failures in Development', *Journal of Economic Perspectives*, Vol.4 (1990).
29. A. Singh, *Public Enterprises in Developing Countries and Economic Efficiency* (UNCTAD, 1992).
30. Colclough, 'Structuralism versus Neoliberalism', p.16.
31. Jenkins, 'Reinterpreting Brazil and South Korea', p.194.
32. See W.J. Baumol, *Business Behaviour, Value and Growth* (New York, 1962).
33. Singh, 'Public Enterprises in Developing Countries'.
34. Ibid.
35. A. Singh, *The Stock Market and Economic Development: Should Developing Countries Encourage Stock Markets?* (UNCTAD, 1992).
36. Singh, 'Public Enterprises in Developing Countries'.
37. Ibid.
38. A. Krueger, 'The Political Economy of the Rent-Seeking Society', *American Economic Review*, Vol.64 (1974); and J.N. Bhagwati, 'Directly Unproductive Profit Seeking Activities', *Journal of Political Economy*, Vol.90 (1982).
39. J. Buchanan, 'Rent Seeking and Profit Seeking', in J. Buchanan, R. Tollison and G. Tullock (eds), *Towards a Theory of the Rent Seeking Society* (Texas, 1980).
40. H.-J. Chang, 'The Political Economy of Industrial Policy: Reflections on the Role of State Intervention', (Cambridge Ph.D., 1991), p.40.
41. Ibid., p.41.
42. Amsden, 'Theory of Government Intervention'.
43. Chang, 'Political Economy of Industrial Policy', p.34.
44. C.H. Moon, 'The Politics of Structural Adjustment in South Korea: Analytical Issues and Comparative Implications', *Korea Journal*, Vol.31 (1991).
45. A. Amsden, 'East Asia's Challenge – to Standard Economics', *The American Prospect* (Summer, 1990), pp.147–8.
46. A. Chowdhury and I. Islam, *The Newly Industrialising Economies of East Asia* (New York, 1993).
47. M.K. Nabli and J.B. Nugent, 'The New Institutional Economics and its Applicability to Development', *World Development*, Vol.17 (1989).
48. Chang, 'Political Economy of Industrial Policy', p.67.
49. H. Leibenstein, 'Organisational Economics and Institutions as Missing Elements in Economic Development Analysis', *World Development*, Vol.17 (1989).
50. Amsden, 'Theory of Government Intervention'.
51. Ibid.
52. Ibid.
53. C. Hamilton, 'Capitalist Industrialisation in East Asia's Four Little Tigers', *Journal of Contemporary Asia*, Vol.13 (1983).
54. K. Lee and H.Y. Lee, 'States, Markets and Economic Development in East Asian Capitalism and Socialism', *Development Policy Review*, Vol.10 (1992).
55. Nabli and Nugent, 'The New Institutional Economics'.
56. R. Wade, 'What Can Economics Learn?' *Annals of the American Academy of Political and Social Science*, No.505 (1989).
57. Amsden, 'Asia's Next Giant', and 'A Theory of Government Intervention'; F. Deyo (ed.), *The Political Economy of the New Asian Industrialism* (Ithaca, 1987); Hamilton, 'Capitalist Industrialisation'.
58. Evans, 'Visible and Invisible Hands', p.56.
59. R. Wade, 'The Role of Government in Overcoming Market Failure: Taiwan, South Korea and Japan', in H. Hughes (ed.), *Achieving Industrialisation in Asia* (Cambridge, 1988).
60. Wade, 'What Can Economics Learn?', p.29.
61. J.N. Bhagwati, *Protectionism* (Cambridge, Mass., 1988).
62. Ibid.
63. Ibid.
64. Chang, 'The Political Economy of Industrial Policy', p.142.
65. Ibid., p.83.
66. Johnson, 'The Industrial Debate Reexamined', *California Management Review*, Vol.xxvii, No.4 (1984).

67. Chang, 'The Political Economy of Industrial Policy', p.85.
68. Ibid., pp.85–6.
69. O.E. Williamson, 'The Logic of Economic Organisation', *Journal of Law, Economics and Organisations*, Vol.4 (1988).
70. F. Hayek, 'Economics and Knowledge', in F. Hayek (ed.), *Individualism and Economic Order* (London, 1949).
71. Chang, 'The Political Economy of Industrial Policy', p.86.
72. Ibid., p.87.
73. Ibid., p.89.
74. Ibid., p.93.
75. Ibid., p.91.
76. Johnson (1984).
77. Chang, 'The Political Economy of Industrial Policy', p.106.
78. Ibid.
79. D. Okimoto, *Between MITI and the Market* (Stanford, 1989) p.23.
80. Ibid., p.50.
81. Chang, 'The Political Economy of Industrial Policy', p.109.
82. M.R. Agosin, *Trade Policy Reform and Economic Performance: A Review of the Issues and Some Preliminary Evidence* (UNCTAD, 1991).
83. Chang, 'The Political Economy of Industrial Policy'.
84. S. Chakravarty and A. Singh, *The Desirable Forms of Economic Openness in the South* (Helsinki, 1988).
85. B. Balassa, 'The Lessons of East Asia Development'.
86. H. Pack and L. Westphal, 'Industrial Strategy and Technological Change: Theory Versus Reality', *Journal of Development Economics*, Vol.22 (1986).
87. See R. Wade, 'The Role of Government in Overcoming Market Failure: Taiwan, South Korea and Japan', in H. Hughes (ed.), *Achieving Industrialisation in Asia* (Cambridge, 1988); and *Governing the Market: Economic Theory and the Role of Government in East Asian Industrialisation* (Princeton, 1990).

Economic Development and the State: Lessons from Singapore

TAN KONG YAM

I: INTRODUCTION

Singapore achieved self-government from British rule in 1959 and independence from Malaysia in 1965. Since 1965, it has achieved remarkable economic progress, averaging 8.9 per cent per year. Rapid economic growth has been accompanied by substantial structural transformation from a regional entrepot of raw materials and manufactured products into a high value-added manufacturing as well as financial and business services hub in the dynamic Asia-Pacific region. By early 1994, the economy is characterised by full employment, high savings and investment rates, a strong fiscal position, a healthy balance of payments, growing external reserves, a strong currency and a low inflation rate (see Table 1). The Singapore economy is also characterised by small territorial size (630 sq km) and population (three million), poor resource endowment, specialised production structure, heavy dependence on foreign direct investment and international trade, as well as high economic vulnerability. These special characteristics dictated Singapore's development strategy in the past three decades, particularly the highly interventionist social and economic policies. They also shaped the objective of developing Singapore as a global city and the recent drive to regionalisation and the export of surplus capital to tap into the growth of the Asia-Pacific economies.

Four distinct periods of growth performance in Singapore may be distinguished. GDP growth accelerated from an annual average rate of 5.5 per cent in 1960–65 to 12.7 per cent in 1966–73, and decelerated to 7.9 per cent in 1974–84. The economy then went into recession in 1985–86 when growth averaged 0.1 per cent. Boosted by real wage cuts as well as robust regional growth, GDP has since averaged 8.7 per cent between 1987 and 1993 (see Table 2).

The first period since independence (1966–73) marked the early industrialisation phase and had the best economic performance. This period was characterised by a concerted effort in attracting foreign direct investment in labour-intensive, export-oriented manufacturing activities that created jobs to combat the serious unemployment problem and political instability. A programme of infrastructural developments, including industrial estate, public utilities, telecommunications and sea-

Tan Kong Yam, National University of Singapore

TABLE 1
SOCIO-ECONOMIC INDICATORS OF SINGAPORE

	1960	1970	1980	1990	1993
GDP, current S$m	2149.6	5804.9	25090.7	66174.5	89006.7
GDP per capita, S$	na	2825.3	9940.6	22111.8	27683.7
Gross national saving/GNP %	-2.4	19.3	34.2	44.9	46.9
GDCF/GNP %	9.5	32.2	42.2	35.1	40.0
Total exports/GNP %	na	81.1	171.4	149.0	134.2
Official foreign reserves (S$m)	na	3097.9	13757.7	48521.3	77866.8
Visitor arrivals (1000s)	na	521.7	2562.1	5322.9	6425.8
Population (1000s)	1646.4	2074.5	2413.9	3002.8	3186.6
Visitor arrivals per population	na	0.3	1.1	1.8	2.0
Population density (persons per km sq)	2831.3	3537.1	3907.0	4743.8	5034.2
Crude birth rate per 1000 population	37.5	22.1	17.1	18.4	17.0
Crude death rate per 1000 population	6.2	5.2	5.2	4.8	4.7
Infant mortality rate per 1000 live births	34.9	20.5	11.7	6.7	5.0
Literacy rate %	na	72.2	84.0	90.1	na
Employed (1000s)	448.6	644.2	1073.4	1537.0	1592.0
Unemployment rate %	4.9	6.0	3.0	1.7	2.7
Inflation rate %	1.2	5.6	8.5	3.4	2.4
S$ exchange rate (per US$)	na	3.1	2.1	,1.8	1.6

Sources: Department of Statistics, *Economic and Social Statistics* (1960–82); *Yearbook of Statistics* (1990); *Monthly Digest of Statistics* (February 1994).

port facilities, was embarked upon. Measures introduced to establish industrial peace as well as monetary and fiscal prudence greatly improved the investment climate. The main thrust to growth came from the rapid expansion of the manufacturing sector (18.1 per cent per year), trade and tourism sectors. Additionally, for the major part of the period, the

TABLE 2

GDP GROWTH AND INFLATION IN SINGAPORE

Years	GDP	Inflation
1960-65	5.5	1.0
1966-73	12.7	3.4
1974-84	7.9	5.4
1985-86	0.1	-0.5
1987-93	8.7	2.4

Sources: Department of Statistics, *Economic and Social Statistics* (1960–82); *Yearbook of Statistics* (1990); Ministry of Trade and Industry, *Economic Survey of Singapore* (1993).

external environment of free trade, expanding world output and export were highly favourable to international trade and investment. This enabled Singapore to reap the full benefits of its outward-looking export oriented development strategy. Both external trade and foreign investment inflows grew rapidly. Rapid economic growth was accompanied by substantial changes in the production structure. The entrepot and commerce sector declined in relative terms following the policy of diversification towards manufacturing, construction, transport and communications as well as financial and business services (see Table 3).

In the second period (1974–84), growth slowed to an annual average rate of 7.9 per cent, but nonetheless remained buoyant by international standards. The end of double digit growth was brought about by the two international oil shocks of 1973–75 and 1979–80, which led to a worsening international economic environment as well as the gradual emergence of supply side constraint in labour force increase and productivity improvement. As the manufacturing sector grew and became more export oriented, the distribution of industries also shifted from labour intensive to capital and skilled intensive industries. Traditional industries such as food and beverages, textiles, and wood products declined in relative importance. Industries which expanded rapidly included chemical products, fabricated metal products, electrical and electronic products and components as well as machinery and precision equipment (see Table 4). Beginning in the early 1970s, as the manufacturing sector was consolidated the services sector began to expand, particularly on the back of the expanding regional economies. In the course of the decade various measures were introduced to promote Singapore as a financial centre by

TABLE 3

SINGAPORE GDP DISTRIBUTION BY SECTORS %, 1960–93

Industry	1960	1970	1980	1990	1993
Agriculture & Mining	3.9	2.7	1.5	0.4	0.2
Manufacturing	11.7	20.2	28.1	27.8	26.2
Utilities	2.4	2.6	2.1	1.8	1.7
Construction	3.5	6.8	6.2	5.3	7.1
Commerce	33.0	27.4	20.9	16.3	16.9
Transport & Communication	13.6	10.7	13.5	12.6	11.5
Financial & Business Services	14.4	16.7	18.9	26.5	27.4
Other Services	17.6	12.9	8.7	·9.5	9.1

Source: Ministry of Trade and Industry, Yearbook of Statistics (1993).

improving upon Singapore's initial advantage of a crucial time zone location. These included the liberalisation of foreign exchange controls, admission of foreign banks, generous fiscal incentives, and manpower training. The assets of offshore banking called Asian Currency Units rose from US$30.5 million in 1968 to US$128.1 billion in 1984. In addition, the main thrust to the expansion of the transport and communications sector came from the expansion of Singapore Airlines, airport and port services as well as telecommunications. The expansion of this sector came largely from public sector activities.

During the third period (1985–86), the Singapore economy went into recession and contracted by 1.6 per cent in 1985. This was the first negative growth since the early 1960s. The recession which resulted from real wage growth outstripping productivity and a strong exchange rate as well as the weakening of regional growth was a rude shock to the government. Realising the overly interventionist role it had played in the labour market, particularly the high wage policy, in spearheading industrial restructuring during 1979–81, the government acted swiftly to cut real wages by about 12 per cent through a cut of 15 percentage points in the social security contribution for the central provident fund.[1] The resulting significant improvement in international competitiveness as well as profitability, together with the external inflow of direct foreign investment, caused the economy to rebound. Growth resumed to 1.8 per cent in 1986

TABLE 4

INDUSTRIAL STRUCTURAL SHIFT IN THE MANUFACTURING SECTOR

MAJOR INDUSTRY GROUP	VALUE ADDED		EMPLOYMENT	
	1974	1984	1974	1984
Food & Beverages	6.7	5.5	6.4	4.9
Textiles	2.4	0.7	5.9	1.4
Wearing Apparel	2.7	3.6	10.2	10.2
Wood Products	2.8	1.0	5.8	1.8
Furniture	0.5	1.2	1.3	2.7
Paper Products and Printing	4.5	6.3	5.6	6.5
Chemical Products	4.6	8.1	2.3	2.8
Petroleum	24.5	8.6	1.5	1.3
Rubber & Plastic Products	2.0	2.4	3.1	3.6
Non-Metallic Minerals	3.0	3.6	2.4	3.0
Basic Metals	3.2	1.5	1.0	0.9
Fabricated Metal Products	4.1	6.8	5.2	7.6
Machinery & Appliances	21.8	39.0	29.5	40.3
Transport Equipment	15.2	9.1	13.8	9.0
Precision Equipment	1.0	1.5	3.9	2.0
Other Products	1.0	1.1	2.1	2.0
Total %	100.0	100.0	100.0	100.0
Total $m	3579.0	11,122.0	209,214.0	275,080.0

Sources: Department of Statistics, *Census of Industrial Production*.

and bounced back to a robust 9.4 per cent by 1987. Since the recovery in 1987, growth has averaged 8.7 per cent. By the end of 1990, Singapore had evolved into a major regional business and financial hub in the dynamic Asia-Pacific region. The end of 1990 also saw the transition of political leadership from Lee Kuan Yew to a new and younger generation of political leaders headed by Goh Chok Tong. The new leadership crystallised the formulation of a comprehensive vision of the long-term strategic development direction of Singapore. Called the 'Next Lap', this vision is for Singapore to attain the status and characteristics of a first league developed country within the next 20–30 years. The specific industrial strategies were fleshed out in the Strategic Economic Plan (SEP) prepared by the Ministry of Trade and Industry (MTI).[2] The key elements in the SEP include: positioning Singapore as a global city or 'total business hub' in the Asia-Pacific region at par with other leading global cities in the world; emphasis on attracting high-tech, knowledge-intensive industries and promoting high-value, innovative and creative activities; intensified investment in developing infrastructures and enhancing human resources; promoting teamwork and cooperation between labour, business and government; and internationalisation of local firms as a means to transcend the constraints of small physical size and to achieve better access to overseas markets and technology.

II: DEVELOPMENTAL STATE-CONCEPTUAL ISSUES

The traditional dominant explanation for the enormous success of the East Asian capitalist economies has been to ascribe it to the efficient resource allocation effect of the free market, economic openness, the provision of a stable macroeconomic environment and a reliable legal framework, 'getting the prices right' and the limited role of the government. Adherents of this neo-classical view included Chen, Patrick, Friedman and Fei.[3] Over the past decade or so, however, a new stream of literature has increasingly emphasised the directive and developmental role of the state in the economic success of East Asia. This revisionist view emphasised the significance of the government–business relationship, resulting in the government not merely being a referee and setting the broad rules of the game, but often acting as a major participant with determining influence on business decisions through direct manipulation of incentives and disincentives in promoting industrial development.[4]

This literature emphasised that international competitive advantage in specific products and industries could be deliberately and purposefully created and nurtured in the relentless process of skill, technology and product upgrading in the course of economic development. While from a short-run and static perspective, these intervention policies in the factor and product markets appeared to conflict with the operation of the free market and economic rationalism, interventions that nurture industries of rapid technological progress, rising labour productivity and high income elasticity of demand could be dynamically efficient from a long-term perspective.[5] This view also emphasised the significance of the numerous formal and informal institutions and channels for consultation and coordination between the elite economic bureaucracy and the private sector in the process of policy formulation, implementation and modification. These interventions using fiscal incentives, socialising of risk and direct credit control mechanisms could result in very high level of productive investment in specific key industries, far higher than would have occurred in the free market situation.[6] Efficiency was maintained, either in ruthless competition among protected domestic firms or eventual exposure to international competition for the industries. The supporting institutional and organisational arrangements in making such interventionist structures possible were soft authoritarianism and corporatist political systems that allow for market guidance.[7]

In the 1993 report on 'East Asian Miracles', the World Bank noted that, since 1960, the eight high performing Asian economies (HPAE) of Japan, Hong Kong, Korea, Taiwan, Singapore, Malaysia, Indonesia and

Thailand have grown at about 5.5 per cent in per capita terms, more than twice as fast as the rest of East Asia (2.4 per cent), and roughly three times as fast as Latin America (1.8 per cent) and South Asia (1.9 per cent), and five times faster than Sub-Sahara Africa. The report noted that the HPAEs maintained important fundamental policies like macroeconomic stability, the principle of shared growth, high savings rate and heavy investments in human capital, stable and secure financial systems, limited price distortion as well as openness to foreign technology. In addition, they actively promoted selective interventions like mild financial repression which kept real interest rates positive but low, directed credit, selective industrial promotion and export promoting trade policies. These interventionist policies were deemed necessary largely because they helped to address the critical problem of a class of market failures, namely coordination failures, particularly in the early stage of development. The complementary key ingredient to ensure success, however, was that the government distributed rewards, often in the form of privileged access to credit or foreign exchange, on the basis of competitive performance rather than rent-seeking activities. Thus selective interventions were disciplined by competition via either markets or contests. In addition, the existence of a high-quality civil service that was insulated from political interference and had the capacity to monitor performance impartially has been crucial to such selective intervention and to contest-based competition.

III: LESSONS FROM SINGAPORE

The economic success of Singapore in the past three decades demonstrated both the power of the neo-classical view and the importance of the revisionist perspective to complement the explanation of high growth. As the neo-classical view correctly pointed out, Singapore's growth was characterised by a high savings rate (34–45 per cent of GDP since the early 1980s), heavy investment in human capital, fiscal and monetary prudence leading to macroeconomic stability, minimal price distortion, stable and secure financial systems and extreme openness to international trade, investment and technology transfer. In addition, as the revisionists stressed, the story of Singapore demonstrated the necessity and capacity of a country with no natural resources to create national competitive advantage through selective industrial promotion and infrastructural development and continuously to renew it in a relentless process of up-grading industrial structure and living standards.

The traditional justification of public sector involvement is that of externalities and other forms of market failure. To the extent that much basic research, manpower training, infrastructural support for national competitive advantage and technology diffusion have public goods characteristics, they create significant positive externalities that cannot be easily appropriated by the investing parties. Consequently, the private sector would tend to under-invest compared to what is deemed socially desirable. Another usual justification for public sector intervention is the failure of the capital market in allocating finance and pooling risks for major R & D projects involving high fixed costs, long time horizon and great uncertainty. On the other hand, public sector involvement may be socially inefficient due to the agency problem, rent seeking by special interest groups, and other sources of government failures.

In the context of Singapore, the government has involved itself as a key player in the economy largely on the justification of weak institutional structure in the early stage of development, coordination failures, positive externalities and perceived pervasive market failures in a small open economy. It assumes the function of factor creator, such as human resource development, investment in research and development and internationally competitive infrastructure in national hardware and software. The approach adopted by the government is often strategic and proactive not *ad hoc* and reactive. The lead time needed in factor creation is frequently taken into account, so institution building often occurs with a view to the future. This creation of national competitive advantage is crucial for Singapore as it has few natural factor endowments besides its human resources and geographic location. Foreign and domestic investments will only stay in Singapore if it is able to offset its natural resource disadvantage with a man-made advantage: superior national infrastructures. In the early stage of development, Singapore's geographic location gave it a natural base to build sea and air transport facilities that served to establish its competitive position as a regional hub for physical production and transport (manufacturing, entrepot trades and distribution), and the recent development of information and tele-communications infrastructure is a logical next step to stengthen further Singapore's role as a regional hub for information production and communication (financial and business services, regional headquarters operations, R & D, design, regional marketing, training and technical support services, and so on).

To assess the success and effectiveness of the government's role in economic development, it is instructive to look at three specific case studies and draw lessons from them. The first case involved an intervention in the labour market by boosting wages to speed up industrial restructuring in the early 1980s. It was a case of major failure in government intervention. The second case involved the creation of national competitive advantage through heavy investment in information-telecommunications infrastructure for the promotion of information technology since the second half of the 1980s. It has proved to be fairly successful so far. The third case was an ambitious National Technology Plan unveiled in 1991 to usher the nation into the innovative phase of development. It entailed a $2 billion research and development fund. The verdict is still out on this ambitious project.

National Wage Policy For Industrial Restructuring

Double digit economic growth in the late 1960s and the beginning of the 1970s reduced the unemployment rate very quickly from over nine per cent in the early 1960s to 4.5 per cent by 1973. Signs of a tight labour market began to emerge in the early 1970s and there was concern that wages might escalate, eroding international competitiveness. The government's response was to establish the National Wage Council (NWC) in 1972, with representation from the employers' federations, trade unions, and government to manage the wage increase process. The NWC, chaired by an academic, served as an independent advisory body to the government with the following objectives: (i) to recommend annual wage increases; (ii) to ensure orderly wage development so as to promote economic and social development; and (iii) to assist in the development of incentive schemes to improve national productivity. The NWC normally recommended nominal wage increases for the entire economy on an annual basis. Table 5 gives a summary of the NWC wage recommendations since 1972. How these guidelines were decided upon was not known as NWC deliberations, arrived at by consensus, were kept confidential. According to published NWC records, the factors taken into consideration in the decisions included

> increases in productivity, changes in the exchange rate and inflation rate, changes in wage structure, the competitive position of Singapore's exports, domestic employment and unemployment situation, balance of payments, foreign investment and world economic condition. The weight given to each factor varies from year to year.[8]

In principle, the wage guidelines of the NWC were not mandatory. They were, however, endorsed by the Cabinet and were followed by the public sector. These recommendations were also widely implemented by the private sector. Various surveys by employers' federations showed that since 1977 at least three-quarters of private-sector employers have 'followed' the NWC recommendations.[9]

In 1979, the government noted that compared to the other newly industrialising economies like Hong Kong, Taiwan and Korea, the upgrading process of Singapore's industrial structure into more capital and skilled intensive products had been slow. Singapore seemed to be stuck in low value-added, labour intensive industries.[10] The response of the government was to use the NWC wage guidelines as an important policy tool in the economic restructuring process. Initiated in 1979, the three-year 'wage correction policy' of high-wage recommendations was designed to raise capital intensity, reduce the reliance on cheap unskilled foreign

TABLE 5

NATIONAL WAGE COUNCIL WAGE RECOMMENDATIONS

Year	Settlement
1972	8%
1973	9%
1974	10% + $40
1975	6%
1976	7%
1977	6%
1978	6% + $12
1979	7% + $32
1980	7.7% + $33 + 3%
1981	6-10% + $32 + 2%
1982	2.5-6.5% + $18.5
1983	2.6% + $10
1984	4-8% + $27
1985	3-7%

Sources: Ministry of Labour, *Yearbook of Statistics*.

TABLE 6

REAL WAGE INCREASES, TOTAL LABOUR COSTS AND PRODUCTIVITY
GROWTH (ALL INDUSTRIES)

	Real Wage Increase	Real Total Labour Costs	Real Productivity Growth
Average 1973-78	1.7	1.2	1.2
Average 1979-81	4.7	7.4	4.8
Average 1982-84	8.3	12.8	4.3

Sources: Department of Statistics, *Yearbook of Statistics* (1985, 1992); Ministry of Labour, *Yearbook of Labour Statistics*.

labour, increase labour productivity and enhance living standards. The NWC recommended nominal wage increases averaging 12.2 per cent for 1980–82. The actual nominal wage increase turned out to be even higher, averaging 14.1 per cent. More significantly, in a tight labour market, expectational factors and institutional rigidity have carried forward the momentum generated by the three-year corrective wage policy so that wage increase continued at over nine per cent for the subsequent years of 1983–84. Coupled with the substantial increase in central provident contributions (CPF) and an increase in other labour costs, the result was an unmitigated disaster. As indicated in Table 6, from 1979 to 1981, during the wage correction period, increases in real total labour costs (wages as well as CPF and other wage-related costs) exceeded productivity growth by an average of 2.6 per cent points per year. However, since 1982, after the wage correction period was supposedly over, this gap between wage and productivity increases widened even further, to 8.5 percentage points per year. This compounded into a 40 per cent increase in unit labour costs over the period 1979–84. As a result, between 1979 and 1984, Singapore's competitive position weakened by 50 per cent against Hong Kong, 15 per cent against Taiwan and 35 per cent against Korea.[11]

In addition, the gross operating surplus of Singapore companies, as a percentage of value-added for the economy as a whole, has fallen by seven percentage points since 1980. The share of wages has increased six percentage points, from 40 per cent of GDP in 1980 to 46 per cent in 1984. As a result, the rate of return on capital in the manufacturing sector has declined steadily, from 33.3 per cent in 1980 to 16.5 per cent in 1984, barely above that of the major OECD countries (see Table 7). The resulting loss in international competitiveness and fall in profitability led to a decline of 38.7 per cent in net investment commitments in the manufacturing sector to $1.1 billion in 1985. Real exports declined by 5 per cent and GDP contracted by 1.6 per cent.

Having enjoyed over eight per cent growth for 20 years, the government was jolted out of its complacency by the recession in 1985. Through the Economic Committee Report, it acted swiftly to reduce labour costs. By April 1986, the employer CPF contribution rate was reduced by 15 percentage points, equivalent to a wage cut of 12 per cent, for a period of

TABLE 7

RATE OF RETURN IN MANUFACTURING

	1980	1984
Singapore	33.3	16.5
Japan	20.5	25.2
USA	12.3	15.8
Germany	13.0	13.7
France	11.5	10.8
Italy	19.2	15.8
UK	5.6	6.7
Canada	13.3	9.9
G7 Average	13.7	15.3

Source: OECD Economic Outlook (June 1985).

two years in the first instance. In addition to the CPF reduction, a period of wage restraint was instituted for 1986 and 1987. The public sector again took the lead on wage cuts and restraint. The resulting improvement in unit labour costs and profitability, coupled with the weakening of the exchange rate between 1986 and 1987, resulted in a substantial inflow of direct foreign investments and a strong recovery of real exports. Net investment commitment in the manufacturing sector rose by 29 per cent in 1986 and a further 20 per cent to reach $1.74 billion in 1987. Real exports increased by 23 per cent and 35 per cent during the same period. Boosted by rising exports and investment, the economy recovered by 1.8 per cent in 1986 and bounced back to 9.4 per cent by 1987.

A significant rethink on the role of the government in active labour market intervention was instituted after the recession. While recognising that NWC recommendations guided wage negotiation, that settlements were swiftly and amicably reached, and that the climate of industrial relations have remained harmonious and non-confrontational, the government noted that the drawbacks of the system had become apparent in the recession, because NWC recommendations have been applied across-the-board to all companies and all workers. Companies which were doing badly settled for higher wage increases than if there had been no NWC recommendations, and therefore suffered the consequences of doing so, while reward was not given to those whose productivity improved more than others. Consequently, the NWC became the cause of wage rigidity in Singapore.[12] Subsequently, a subcommittee of the NWC was formed to look into the issue of wage reform. Their proposals were announced in mid-November 1986. Their recommendation was that the wage structure should comprise a basic wage to reflect the value of the job and to provide a measure of stability to the workers' income; an annual wage supplement of one month's basic wage which may be adjusted under exceptional circumstances; and a variable performance bonus based on company performance, to be paid yearly or half-yearly. In addition, there should be a small service increment of about two per cent which could either be negotiated annually or fixed for the duration of the collective agreement. The variable bonus could be based on either a profit-sharing system, and/or a productivity system. There would be a five-year phasing-in period, during which the subcommittee recommended that the NWC provide guidelines on the total wage cost increase for the economy, based on national productivity, economic performance, inflation and international competitiveness. These proposals were endorsed by union leaders and employers' federations.[13]

Creating National Competitive Advantage in Information-Telecommunications Infrastructure

The rapid diffusion of the application of Information Technology (IT) means that a new order of the international division of labour is evolving.

National competitive advantage in information-telecommunications infrastructure, both at the hardware and software level, particularly the rapid accessibility of information and the ability to process and use the results speedily to sharpen the competitive edge of enterprises and nations, will increasingly determine the new international hierarchy of nations. IT provides the rapid capability to integrate design, manufacturing, procurement, sales, and administrative and technical support services in any enterprise. With the geographical dispersion of production, procurement, design, sales and marketing from overall headquarter location, the urgent need to have centralised coordination in a physical location at a geographical zone has become more imperative for major MNCs in the world. An efficient and cost effective national information-telecommunications infrastructure thus becomes critical for a regional business services centre like Singapore. In particular, an efficient information-telecommunications infrastructure helps to reduce transaction costs, leading to improved efficiency in existing intra-organisational operations as well as prevailing external market exchanges. In addition, it enhances value creation, enabling new products and services to be delivered and new value-creating processes to be performed that were previously not possible.

The IT sector in Singapore, defined as encompassing activities associated with the production and dissemination of information goods and services, has been identified as a key industry since the 1980s. There is a multi-agency exercise for developing and promoting information-telecommunications infrastructure and development. Apart from the direct telecommunications facilities offered by Singapore Telecom, the other statutory body which has been actively promoting IT and related computerisation activities is the National Computer Board (NCB) which was established in 1980. The comprehensive National Information Technology Plan (NITP) was developed by the NCB and other public agencies as a blueprint for all aspects of IT development in Singapore in 1986. The plan included specific objectives and deadlines for training people; creating an IT culture; enhancing the communications infrastructure; generating and supporting IT applications; fostering a world-class indigenous IT industry that includes software, hardware and computer services; and pioneering new information technology applications through R & D.

Since 1986, the implementation of the NITP has achieved significant success. The Civil Service Computerization Programme has been successfully implemented and extended to the private sector to evolve a nation-wide information system. National electronic data interchange (EDI) networks including TradeNet, MediNet, BuildNet, and LawNet, have been established. A wide array of IT training institutions are developing specialists in communications, integrated manufacturing, artificial intelligence and software engineering. A particularly notable success story of creating national competitive advantage through an efficient information-telecommunications infrastructure has been the implementation of TradeNet. Initiated by the government and run by Singapore Network Services (SNS) since 1 January 1989, TradeNet has been an unqualified success in helping to manage Singapore's huge external trade of $257 billion a year – 2.9 times the GNP. It has helped to save Singaporean traders an estimated one billion US dollars a year. International trade has traditionally involved an enormous amount of paperwork. With TradeNet, however, traders simply fill out one electronic form, which can be submitted by modem to the Trade Development Board's main computer 24 hours a day. Information is then routed, again electronically, to the appropriate government agencies from among the 18 involved in issuing trade documents. Approvals, often generated with the help of expert systems, are deposited in the electronic mailbox of the trader, typically within 15 minutes. To reduce paperwork further, application fees and custom duties are automatically debited from the the trader's bank through electronic funds transfer. TradeNet also automatically routes approved permits to the Port and Civil Aviation Authorities to facilitate the physical clearance of goods. As part of the information-telecommunications competitive infrastructure, the expert systems for container planning, a system called PortNet was developed to synergise with TradeNet. This system allows for the electronic declaration of vessel calls, electronic data interchange links with other ports for processing arriving ships, and artificial-intelligence-based pattern recognition systems that automatically encode container numbers.

The next phase of Singapore's strategy is aimed at transforming commercial, financial, business services and society to create an 'intelligent island'. The government has dubbed this new plan 'IT 2000'.[14] Singapore proposes to build a National Information Infrastructure which will enable the national information, communication and transaction system to work. In this case, Singapore's small size has been turned into an advantage. The physical infrastructure needed to support the information age can be more easily put in place in a country of Singapore's dimensions. Singapore is thus poised to become the world's first fully networked society – one in which all homes, schools, businesses, and government agencies will be interconnected in an electronic grid. It represents what can happen when a government assumes an instrumental position in actively shaping and investing in creating national competitive advantage. And it underscores the importance of identifying and investing in certain key capabilities. There are very few inherent competitive advantages that nations and corporations can continuously count on. Advantages thus have to be created and continuously renewed. Singapore has leveraged its single natural advantage of strategic location by establishing world-class transportation systems and materials handling facilities; and extended such 'hubbing' into the financial and other business services activities by establishing a sophisticated communications and information technology infrastructure. Singapore now positions itself as a 'value-added switching node' and a gateway in the dynamic Asia-Pacific region.

The importance of information-telecommunications infrastructure in supporting Singapore's competitive advantage as a regional financial and business centre has been confirmed by successive rounds of international surveys of business leaders as reported in the annual World Competitive Report. In the 1992 Report, for example, Singapore's telecommunications infrastructure was given a rating of 97.5 out of 100, which not only topped the league of newly industrialising nations, but was also ahead of some of the OECD countries. The Singapore government clearly recognises that its competitive advantage lies not in creating new technologies, but in rapid exploitation and application of technologies already developed elsewhere. This fast follower strategy emphasised the building up of the nation's technology absorption capacity – the effectiveness of scanning, learning, assimilating and possibly improving upon available technology created by others to gain competitive advantage, while leaving the task of risky exploration of new technologies to more advanced nations with far greater resources.[15] Singapore's drive to create an information, networked society has a built-in dilemma: there is an inherent conflict between the democratisation of information creation and access and the government's long-standing concern to control the information its citizens receive for fear of undermining national values. It would not be too presumptuous to surmise that eventually the democratisation of information creation and access will gradually undermine the government's control on information in a fully networked society.

National Technology Plan

For the past 30 years, Singapore has gradually moved from a low wage production base to a high value-added manufacturing and services hub in the Asia-Pacific region. Increasingly, its labour has become too expensive relative to that of the regional economies which are fast catching up in skill, technology and managerial expertise. To sustain competitiveness, Singapore needs to move to an innovation phase of development and promote activities with more innovative and design content. Consequently, Singapore must increase her capacity to undertake research and development of international standard. This process has already begun but has been somewhat slow. For example, national expenditure on R & D increased from $38 million or 0.2 per cent of GDP in 1978 to $460 million or 1.0 per cent of GDP in 1990. Private sector spending on R & D expanded from $26 million in 1978 to $380 million in 1990. The private sector therefore accounted for more than half of the total national expenditure on R & D by 1990. In 1978, Singapore had only 1,672 people working in R & D; by 1990, this number had risen to 7,004. The number of research scientists and engineers (RSEs) as a proportion of the labour force had also risen from eight per 10,000 in 1978 to 28 per 10,000 by 1990.[16] However, Singapore is still a long way behind the world leaders or the other NIEs. Other economies like the US, Europe, Japan, Taiwan and Korea all have plans to boost science and technology. Korea, which now spends about 1.8 per cent of its GDP on R & D, has developed a detailed plan to raise its level of R & D spending to five per cent of GDP by the year 2000. Taiwan, which spends 1.3 per cent of its GDP on R & D, plans to increase it to two per cent in the 1990s. Similarly, while the number of research scientists and engineers (RSEs) per 10,000 labour force in Singapore rose from 29 in 1990 to 37 in 1992, it is still sub-stantially lower than the other NIEs like that of Taiwan (54), Korea (40), let alone the more developed countries like Japan (91), the US (69), Germany (58), France (51) and the UK (46).[17] Realising the severe competition from the other NIEs who are ahead in promoting science and technology and to uplift the state of Singapore's science and technology base, the government formed the National Science and Technology Board (NSTB) in early 1991 with the mission to develop Singapore into a centre of excellence in selected fields of science and technology, so as to enhance national competitiveness in the industrial and services sectors. The NSTB published a National Technology Plan called the 'Window of Opportunities' in September 1991.

Realising the limited capacity for a small economy to undertake basic research, the National Technology Plan concentrated on that part of research directed towards economic upgrading. Thus, Singapore's science and technology research would have to be result-driven and it must produce results eventually relevant to economic upgrading and competitiveness. In order to be successful in 'industry-driven' R & D, the government realised that the private sector must undertake the bulk of these activities, because the best measure of the value of such R & D activities would be the willingness of profit-seeking organisations to commit funds and resources to it. Realising the effect of high fixed costs, long time horizons and great uncertainty in hindering private sector investment in R & D, the government felt that, by sharing part of this extra cost and risk, it would encourage more private sector R & D, and foster national competitiveness and economic vigour. Thus the government decided that it should play a more proactive coordinating and facilitating role to promote these efforts. Its role was to gauge what resources companies needed in order to under-take more R & D and then to find the means of providing the support. The specific targets set out in the National Technology Plan were for total national expenditure on R & D to reach two per cent of GDP by 1995, a minimum 50 per cent private sector share of this total, and a ratio of the number of scientists and engineers engaged in R & D activities of 40 per 10,000 labour force by 1995.

To achieve these specific targets, the National Technology Plan set out the main thrusts that government would take in the next five years to achieve these targets, and how it intended to provide the environment that would support active and widespread R & D by companies in Singapore. The key recommendations were:

- A $2 billion Research & Development Fund to support industry-driven R & D over the next five years;
- Provision of grants and fiscal incentives to encourage more R & D by the private sector.
- Assistance in developing and recruiting R & D manpower, domestically and overseas.
- Support and funding for research centres and institutes that can train the manpower or provide the technological support to enable companies to undertake their R & D; and
- Assistance for commercialisation and infrastructural support.

More specifically, research and development expenditures and priorities would be focused on the following technologies: information technology, microelectronics, electronics system, manufacturing technology, materials technology, energy, water, environment and resources, biotechnology, food and agrotechnology as well as medical services. The NSTB has proposed several ways to use tax incentives to promote R & D: the extension of pioneer status up to an additional two years for companies that are prepared to undertake specified R & D activities in Singapore, similar extension of post-pioneer concessions, double deduction for R & D expenses, accelerated depreciation for capital expenditure incurred in acquiring approved know-how or patent rights, and tax exemptions for incremental income earned and for R & D reserves. In addition to fiscal incentives, the plan proposed to attract more Singaporeans into R & D and to supplement this with research talent from overseas. The government helped to defray part of the training costs through the provision of scholarships and financial aid as well as specific grants.

More importantly, successful commercial exploitation of R & D required the ability to bring together other assets such as finance or capital, marketing skills, distribution network, and competitive manufacturing capabilities. Start-ups typically have difficulties commercialising their research findings because they do not possess, or cannot find, all the requisite elements. The NSTB was also tasked to assist start-ups by helping to bring the elements together. For example, administrative policies could be changed and institutional barriers removed to encourage greater tie-ups between the research institutes and industry. If finance or managerial expertise were lacking, the NSTB could also assist in matchmaking these with R & D start-ups through strategic partnerships, joint ventures, or direct equity investments in the start-ups. In short, the aim was for the NSTB to develop into a 'one-stop Technology Assistance Centre' covering the entire life cycle of R & D.

It is still too early to assess the relative success of the Singapore government's role in fostering R & D in sustaining competitiveness. There were, however, some indications that things were moving in the correct direction. The R & D survey in 1993 indicated that Singapore spent a total of $894.9 million on research and development in 1992, up from $756.8 million in 1991. This meant that R & D spending was 1.2 per cent of the GDP, indicating that Singapore was on schedule to reach its goal of two per cent R & D expenditure by 1995. The number of research scientists and engineers also rose from 34 per 10,000 in the labour force in 1991 to 37 per 10,000 in 1992. There were some indications that some private companies were beginning to build up core industrial capabilities in key technologies. Examples included the many public sector bodies which have developed such capabilities, such as the Institute of Systems Science which was recently selected as one of four foreign partners in the Japan Real World Computing Sixth Generation Initiative. And, in the private sector, Hewlett Packard's R & D team in Singapore developed its first colour inkjet and portable printer. Motorola's local team was responsible for a credit-card sized pager and other telecommunication products. In addition, more strategic alliances between private companies and public sector organisations, and between Singapore and other countries were being formed. The Glaxo-Institute of Molecular & Cell Biology Centre set up in early 1993 and the Apple-Institute of Systems Science Centre set up in 1992 were examples.[18]

IV: CONCLUSION

It is clear from the above analysis and case studies that the intervention experience of the Singapore government in fostering economic development has not always been successful. In the case of the high wage policy, it was an unmitigated disaster, though it was to the credit of the government that corrective measures were undertaken fairly rapidly so that the ensuing recession lasted only about one and a half years. In justifying government intervention to foster economic development, a key rationale is the existence of an imperfect market and incomplete information, leading to pervasive market failure. As noted by Stiglitz,[19] while traditional literature characterises market failures as exceptions to the general rule that decentralised markets lead to efficient allocation, in the new view the presumption is reversed. It is only under exceptional circumstances that markets are efficient. This makes the analysis of the appropriate role of government far more difficult as the issue becomes one not of identifying market failures but of identifying large market failures where there is scope for significant welfare-enhancing government interventions.

In the case of Singapore, the unique feature of smallness and compact size could have made government intervention more effective and manageable, leading to less government failure. In addition, being small, the law of large numbers does not apply as readily and hence it can be argued that pervasive market failure for competitive factor and product markets calls for a more interventionist approach. It is, however, significant to note that the emphasis on government intervention in Singapore is largely geared towards production rather than consumption or re-distribution. Instead of intervening or deploying resources to create a welfare state, the emphasis of intervention was in actively creating national competitive advantages through infrastructural investments, R & D subsidy, and manpower development to strengthen long-term productive capability.

Government interventions in the factor market have been more controversial and have not produced expected success. For example, intervention in the labour market has proved to be counter-productive. In addition, some interventions in the capital market, like the central provident fund forced savings scheme that led to a savings and investment rate of above 40 per cent of GDP, has resulted in weak capital productivity and poor total factor productivity performance.[20] It is noteworthy that the public sector in Singapore is strong, non-corrupt and run in a much more commercial manner compared to that of most other countries. Civil servants have a market-oriented evaluation and reward system, with a bonus and performance system built in. In addition, the public sector as a whole has its annual bonus tied to the overall performance of the economy. With the public sector's bottom line tied directly to fostering economic growth, the incentive system has been able to galvanise the public sector in servicing private sector interest in growth and development. In addition, the market based system has also significantly injected market rationality into public sector intervention, helping to avoid large and wasteful public sector projects, as well as vast rent-seeking activities. Hence, interventions tend to be more market facilitating, correcting and enhancing rather than distorting. In addition, Singapore has the advantage of a small open economy constantly under the check of international competitive forces, so that policies or interventions that are too market distorting would be fairly rapidly overwhelmed by international competitive forces.

The cultural element that facilitates government intervention and leadership in East Asia is the greater emphasis on the interest of the group, community or state over that of the individual. Under this cultural milieu, it is considerably easier for the government to harness resources and mobilise the private sector to pursue major development goals, more so when the process of recruitment of the public sector allows it to capture a large share of the best and dedicated minds in the country. It is not clear, however, whether some of the success in government intervention in Singapore and the other NIEs are merely a function of their stage of development. As a follower in the process of economic catching up, it is not as difficult in identifying priorities in industry, infrastructure investment, R & D expenditure, and manpower development. However, as the case of Japan shows, when these countries gradually reach the technological frontier and are also in the process of pushing forward the frontier, the same policy success of government intervention could no longer be replicated.

NOTES

1. See Ministry of Trade and Industry, *Report on the Economic Committee. The Singapore Economy: New Directions* (Singapore, 1986).
2. The author was a participant in the two-year exercise in drawing up the SEP. This exercise in the Strategic Economic Plan is similar to the close consultation and deliberation between the elite economic bureaucracy and the private sector in the process of policy formulation as emphasised by the revisionist school of thought. See C. Johnson, *MITI and the Japanese Miracle: The Growth of Industrial Policy, 1925–75* (Stanford, 1982).
3. E.K.Y. Chen, *Hyper-Growth in Asian Economies: A Comparative Study of Hong Kong, Japan, Korea, Singapore and Taiwan* (London, 1979); H. Patrick, 'The Future of the Japanese Economy: Output and Labour Productivity', *Journal of Japanese Studies* (1977); M. Friedman and R. Friedman, *Free to Choose: A Personal Statement* (New York, 1980); J.C.H. Fei, 'Evolution of Growth Policies of NICs in a Historical and Typological Perspective', Conference Paper, Conference on Patterns of Growth and Structural Change in Asia's Newly Industrialising Countries and Near-NICs in the Context of Economic Interdependence, 1983.
4. E. Mason *et al.*, *The Economic and Social Modernization of the Republic of Korea* (Harvard, 1980); C. Johnson, 'Introduction: The Taiwan Model' in J. Hsiung *et al.* (eds.), *Contemporary Republic of China: The Taiwan Experience* (New York, 1981); and 'MITI and the Japanese Miracle'.
5. Johnson, 'MITI and the Japanese Miracle'; G. White, *Developmental States in East Asia* (London, 1988).
6. A. Amsden, *Asia's Next Giant: South Korea and Late Industrialisation* (Oxford, 1989).
7. Johnson, 'MITI and the Japanese Miracle'; R. Wade, *Governing the Market: Economic Theory and the Role of Government in East Asian Industrialization* (Princeton, 1991).
8. National Wage Council, *Information Booklet* (Singapore, 1978 and 1992).
9. For a more extensive discussion of the extent of implementation of the NWC guidelines, see Chew Soon Beng, 'Income Policies: The Singapore Experience', Conference Paper, Conference on Incomes Policy, Singapore, 1983.
10. See Ministry of Trade and Industry, *Economic Survey of Singapore* (Singapore, 1979).
11. MIT, *Report on Economic Committee*, p.43.
12. See the speech by Mr Lee Hsien Loong in *The Straits Times*, 23 Sept. 1985.
13. See Ministry of Labour, *Report of the National Wages Council Subcommittee on Wage Reform* (Singapore, 1986).
14. National Computer Board, *A Vision of an Intelligent Island – The IT 2000 Report* (Singapore, 1992).
15. P.K. Wong, *Economic Growth and Information-Telecommunications Infrastructures in Singapore* (Singapore, 1992).
16. National Technology Plan (1991).

17. The World Competitiveness Report (1993).
18. See speech by the Minister of Trade and Industry in *The Straits Times*, 3 Sept. 1993.
19. Stiglitz (1989).
20. A.A. Young, *A Tale of Two Cities: Factor Accumulation and Technical Change in Hong Kong and Singapore* (1993); M.H. Toh and L. Low, *Total Factor Productivity in Singapore: Some Myths and Issues* (1992).

The State and Business Relations in Taiwan

HSIN-HUANG MICHAEL HSIAO

I: INTRODUCTION

In the decade of the 1980s, three major approaches have emerged in the literature of East Asian development studies. Each of the three approaches has centred on one context or agent that is believed to have played a critical role in the development process of East Asia. The first is the global political economy approach that takes the world economy as the crucial external context, and it has incorporated East Asia into the global market from which East Asia has profited. It is a sort of revised world system model in that a peripheral state dependent on a core state within the world economy is not necessarily doomed to be underdeveloped. Rather the dependency could be 'managed' and 'made beneficial' to the ascent of a peripheral state. The second approach takes the state seriously in its role of steering and guiding development strategies and policies to meet the challenge from the global political economic system. The state is being viewed as active and interventionist on both external and internal economic activities. The question of the relative autonomy of the state *vis-à-vis* the dominant local class and other sectors of the society in embarking national development policies is the most discussed topic. The relationship between the state and market forces is also much stressed. Finally, the debate of whether or not authoritarianism is a necessary evil for economic development is another much contested issue. The third approach, compared with the previous two, is a rather new focus in East Asian development studies, and calls our attention to another important agent of capitalist development, the business sector, and the role it has been playing in the course of East Asian development.

It is quite convincing to argue for a new look at the business approach if the picture of East Asian development is to be complete, as business is the central actor in any capitalist development. Aided by favourable timing and external linkages with the global economy and the fact that the active developmental states have responded positively and forcefully to the world system, the success story of East Asia still cannot be fully told if the business chapter is missing. The essence of this business approach should look into questions of how the different sectors within business have 'responded' differently to the state strategies and/or the world market opportunities at the beginning and then later, in turn, 'reshaped' the course of capitalist development and political change in East Asia.

H.-H.M. Hsiao, Academia Sinica, Taipei

The purpose of this paper is to take this approach in order to re-examine Taiwan's post-war economic development experience, and specifically to tackle the following three aspects of this experience. First, the relations between the state and business and the political economic contexts in which the state has been interacting with the different sectors of business in Taiwan. Second, the mechanisms employed by the state to strengthen its links with business, the response of business and how the two actors' interactions have been institutionalised and stabilised in the course of Taiwan's capitalist development. Third, the recent transformation of state–business relations and the sociopolitical forces behind the changes, and the future prospects and implications for Taiwan's further sociopolitical development.

II: THE STATE AND PRIVATE CAPITAL IN TAIWAN

Taiwan's political economic structure has for a long time been characterised by a strong and authoritarian yet developmental state and a large number of politically weak yet economically dynamic small and medium businesses alongside an ever more powerful big business sector. This structure has existed since Taiwan began its export-oriented industrialisation (EOI) in the 1960s. The nature of Taiwan's KMT authoritarian developmental state was established in different phases. The authoritarian rule of the KMT state was already firmly established in Taiwan before state-led rapid industrialisation took shape in the 1960s. It is basically a Leninist state in which the party and state are often indistinguishable, the party often having parallel organisations to the state. Moreover, Taiwan has been controlled by only one party, the KMT, since 1949. In this paper, the term 'state' will be used to indicate the overlap between government and party. The state has also chartered a limited, hierarchical and subordinated set of corporatist structures in civil society, giving them a monopoly to represent various occupational or civil interests, and, therefore, the state has been able to maximise compliance and obedience in civil society under its authoritarian corporatist rule.

Export-oriented industrial development further perpetuated the political authoritarianism over all aspects of civil socity, certainly including the business sector. In other words, unlike Latin America, Taiwan's bureaucratic authoritarianism was not deliberately established for enacting the state-led export promotion strategies, but was rather a pre-existing structure. The dynamic and impressive industrial growth then in turn legitimised the state's powerful authoritarian rule. On the other hand, the business sector as a whole was first nurtured and boosted in the post-land reform import substitution industrialisation (ISI) and it has been more or less subjected to the state's corporatist control since the 1950s. The first generation of local businessmen was created in the 1950s alongside a group of textile industrialists moving from the mainland, and then the first generation of domestic export entrepreneurs evolved in the 1960s. Since the 1970s, the big capitalists that have dominated the domestic market and a great many small and medium entrepreneurs concentrating on the foreign markets have constituted Taiwan's private business sector.

It is no exaggeration to say that both the big capitalists and the small and medium businessmen were in fact the products of the state's leadership in executing the consequential industrialisation strategies in response to both the internal and external political economic challenges. The land reform policy that produced a part of the first generation of indigenous capitalists in Taiwan was forcefully implemented by the KMT regime to ensure its political control over the then agrarian Taiwanese society. The first ISI strategy, in the 1950s, was adopted primarily to meet domestic economic needs and to build local industrial capabilities, and the main beneficiaries of such a strategy were the state-owned enterprises, the mainlander-owned industries and the emerging Taiwanese landlords-turned-capitalists, as well as a few local entrepreneurs who quickly responded to the state's industrial initiatives.

The export-oriented industrialisation (EOI) strategies that followed the first ISI phase then fostered an even larger number of local business enterprises. It witnessed a significant rise in Taiwanese small and medium export-directed enterprises existing side by side with those ever-growing-in-scale larger business sectors controlled by both mainlanders and Taiwanese established during the previous ISI phase. The strategic shift from ISI to EOI, though not necessarily a clear-cut one, was induced and pushed forward by domestic market constraints, external US pressure, and the expected expansion of the world market.[1] The global market provided new opportunities and the state response turned out to be favourable to Taiwan's later development course. The result was the emergence of a dynamic export manufacturing sector large in total output yet small in operational scale. What should be pointed out is that under the protectionist policy of ISI and the state's political manoeuvres with regard to business, the existing big businesses, already enjoying an oligopolistic position in the domestic market, were not interested in expanding into uncontrollable and non-protected foreign markets. It was the rising small and medium businesses which stepped into the 'breach' and fulfilled the 'call' from the state's EOI initiatives. The resulting large numbers of small and medium businesses aiming at the world market should not be interpreted as a conscious and intended policy consequence that had been planned by the state. They were not 'encouraged' by systematic and effective policies as mistakenly portrayed in the recent World Bank Report.[2] Rather it reflected the unequal division of labour in the unique political economy of Taiwan that was dominated by the KMT state and its protected big business and the state-owned enterprises supplying the domestic market. In other words, the newly emerging export market with high competition and without the state's direct guarantee was left in the hands of those small and medium businessmen who, originally left behind, then saw the world market as the only opportunity. The 'dichotomous or dual market structure' was rooted in Taiwan's political economy in the late 1960s.[3]

One other important external contextual factor that unintentionally produced such a dual market (business) structure emanated from the core states, particularly the US. In the late 1950s, the US interest in Taiwan was intensified by the economic recession and worsening balance of payments in the American economy. Overseas markets for American capital seemed to be vital.[4] Moreover, the scarce and increasingly expensive unskilled labour force in the US pushed US buyers to search out low-cost suppliers with cheaper labour costs in lower income countries like Taiwan.[5] The US firms and capitalists with their greater efficiency could also drive out the competition in unprotected markets. With the aim of undermining the ISI model, USAID and the World Bank began to formulate the EOI strategy, encouraging Third World countries to employ their reserves of plentiful and cheap labour to produce low-tech manufactured goods such as textiles, garments, and shoes for export to advanced country markets, where their low labour costs would give them a competitive advantage.[6] A series of policy recommendations were therefore urged by the World Bank and the US. Taiwan was one of the countries directly pressured by USAID and it began a process of structural reform by issuing the 'Nineteen-Point Financial Reforms' in the late 1950s and early 1960s. Included in the package were devaluing of the currency to make exports more competitive, relaxing control over foreign trade, allowing the entry of foreign direct investment to set up export manufacturing enterprises, and initiating a single exchange rate along with eliminating import restrictions. In 1960, 'The Statute for Encouragement of Investment' was issued in order to offer greater tax reductions to stimulate private investment and exports. Moreover, Taiwan's EOI strategy coincided with the needs of US multinational enterprises in the 1960s which saw the opportunity to move their operations to Taiwan to take advantage of local cheap labour to export manufactured products back to the US and to other world markets. These re-export activities of US firms had a dual purpose: to gain a higher return rate on their investment by lowering labour costs; and to compete with Japanese imports such as television sets, micro-chips, and computer goods in the US market.[7]

Foreign direct investment from the US and Japan in Taiwan fostered a wide range of supporting small and medium enterprises that saw the opportunity to take advantage of the newly emerged export promotion policies of the state. One other arrangement that helped accelerate small and medium manufacturers was the so-called 'OEM' (original equipment manufacturer) strategies adopted by the US investors, whereby local manufacturers were assigned to make products which were later sold under US names. Taiwan has been a subcontracting centre since the 1970s, when this sophisticated institutionalised arrangement was established. In fact, its dynamic export performance was, for the most part, due to the work of those OEM factories that constituted the bulk of Taiwan's local small and medium enterprises.[8] The dual business structure, therefore, should be understood within the above-mentioned internal and external contexts, especially the nature of state–business relations and pressure from the World Bank, the US government, and the multinational corporations.

In the early 1970s, faced with the loss of its seat in the UN and the oil crisis, Taiwan experienced a serious setback in economic performance. The drop in business confidence and the outflow of capital brought about a temporary halt to export dynamism, and the diplomatic setback even led to a legitimacy crisis in the KMT state. Taiwan then began the second phase of the ISI strategy to remodel its domestic industrial structure by developing energy-intensive and capital-intensive industries and large-scale infrastructure projects. Under the second phase ISI, state enterprises increased their significance, leading domestic investment, while big businesses received an even greater boost from the state and became 'business groups', the Taiwanese version of the conglomerate. Small and medium businesses, on the other hand, survived the world energy crisis and recession at the time and were re-energised for further growth and development from the late 1970s. From the 1980s, Taiwan's political economic structure of state–private capital relations has been deepened, though it also underwent transformations.

Without doubt, the state has been the dominant force in Taiwan's economy, and, under its effective political and policy mechanisms, both big business and small and medium sectors were created. The domination of the economy by the state not only took the form of hands-on direction and guidance of the business sector as in South Korea; in Taiwan, the state has also actually owned a massive segment of the economy, controlling a significant number of public and KMT party-owned business operations. On top of this, the state owned about 70 per cent of the island's land. Below are more detailed portraits of the relative weight of Taiwan's three business sectors, state and party enterprises, big business, and the small and medium sector.

III: THE PORTRAYAL OF TAIWAN'S BUSINESS SECTOR

The State and the Party Enterprises

Most of Taiwan's state-owned enterprises originated from Japanese *zaibatsu* and Japanese colonial government enterprises which were then taken over by the ROC government after it resumed control of Taiwan following World War Two. Later, more state controlled enterprises were established. In 1952, state businesses accounted for as much as 57 per cent of total industrial production, and 43 per cent of domestic capital formation, and it employed 17 per cent of Taiwan's civilian employees. It was only after the completion of the first phase of ISI in 1960 that public enterprise industrial output fell behind that of private business for the first time, when the figure dropped to 48 per cent, their share of the domestic capital formation to 34 per cent, and the portion of the labour force employed to 11 per cent. In the mid-1970s, when EOI was replaced by second phase ISI, the state enterprises once again received a big boost from the state. Though their share of overall industrial production dropped steadily to 22 per cent, they still contributed 43 per cent of domestic capital formation and employed 12 per cent of Taiwan's labour force. In the late 1980s, the state enterprises accounted for below 20 per cent of Taiwan's industrial production, their average share of the domestic capital formation was about 22 per cent and they hired under ten per cent of Taiwan's total employment.[9]

It is true that the relative weight of state enterprises in Taiwan's economy has been declining over the past four decades, judged by the above figures. However, the significance of its involvement in the economy has grown in magnitude. The heavy penetration of the state in such key sectors as petroleum, electric power, steel, gas, railways, shipbuilding, postal and telecommunication, tobacco and spirits, and banking and other financial segments have all reached monopoly level, and the nature of state and bureaucratic capitalism as reflected by such state dominance in these crucial sectors was quite evident.[10] As late as 1990, ranked according to sales, four of the top ten businesses were state-owned, and the largest private firm, Nan-Ya Plastics, was outstripped by three state enterprises (China Petroleum, Taiwan Tobacco and Wine Monopoly Bureau, and China Steel). Ranking the top ten firms by assets in 1990, six were state-owned. Moreover, state enterprises have also diversified their investments into 40 large private business and seven foreign firms in Taiwan.[11] Thus, the state sector can also, in fact, control the directions of those firms in which they have invested.

In addition to the direct control of the state business sector, the ruling party KMT owns wholly or partly around 50 companies, mostly through the two powerful and privileged party-owned investment firms. These party-owned companies include communications, petrochemicals, steel, and electronics, and extend even to finance and securities.[12] The later development of joint ventures of party investment firms and the state enterprises with the big private companies has even further empowered the party's penetration into the private sector. What has emerged is a new kind of party–state–private capital bloc, which is free from bureaucratic supervision and enjoys a great deal of special favours from the state through political manipulation.[13] According to unofficial estimates, about half of the total assets of Taiwan's corporations are controlled directly or indirectly by the state and the party.[14]

The Big Businesses (Business Groups)

As mentioned earlier, at the end of the first phase of ISI, several big private enterprises emerged with direct state assistance. US aid was used to advance the interests of KMT-linked mainlander businesses of Shanghai and Shantung origins and a few local Taiwanese landlords turned entrepreneurs. With profits guaranteed by a closed market and costs subsidised, mainlander-owned enterprises were the chief beneficiaries of the state's ISI initiatives. They became the upper level of the business power structure in the period prior to 1960. Of the top 21 mainlander-controlled business groups, 15 were long established before 1960. Even in 1981, among the top ten private business groups, three were mainlander-owned (Far Eastern, Yue Loong and Pacific Electric Wire). The first generation of Taiwanese landlords turned capitalists that forged political ties to the KMT state was another business segment that benefited directly from the state's ISI and EOI strategies in the 1950s and 1960s. In most cases, the big Taiwanese business groups were formed under KMT patronage. They were later joined by another type of Taiwanese industrialist, Formosa Plastic's Y.C. Wang, who made a quick response to the opportunities presented by the state's industrial priorities and was greatly assisted by US aid in the early 1960s. The Taiwanese gradually topped the mainlanders to assume the dominant role in Taiwan's private big business sector. Toward the end of the 1980s, among the 97 private business groups (multi-company establishments) in Taiwan, 75 were Taiwanese owned, 13 were in the hands of the mainlanders, and the remaining nine were jointly controlled.[15]

The KMT state has constantly been ambivalent towards the Taiwanese big business groups, and there has always been an ethnic tension between the mainlander state and Taiwanese businesses. There were fears on the part of the KMT state of Taiwanese ambitions for self-determination and independence if they were excessively empowered politically and economically. It was not idle speculation to say that during the second ISI phase in the 1970s, the ethnic power struggle between the state and the Taiwanese economic interests was a consideration when the state enterprises were given a dominant role in leading major industrial projects. Though the rationale given by the state was that private capital did not have the capability to make the huge investment needed to support accelerated industrial expansion, the unspoken reason was that the KMT wished to solve its legitimacy crisis and resume its economic domination by boosting the state-controlled sector. Behind this move was the mainlander-controlled state's efforts to continue to exercise strategic direction of the island's economy with regard to the up-and-coming private capital controlled by the Taiwanese business class.[16] One other political mechanism to keep the Taiwanese business class in check was co-option by recruiting many rising Taiwanese elites or their sons to run for political office. It was indeed a calculated effort in the late 1970s to cement the political links between the KMT state and the Taiwanese business class. Big Taiwanese businesses have been linked with their mainlander counterparts through joint investments and positions in the governing boards of trade associations and other business organisation.[17] The Taiwanese and mainlander divide in big businesses will gradually be eliminated, and they will certainly merge into an ever more powerful capitalist interest bloc.

In 1988, the top 100 business groups of Taiwan accounted for 34 per cent of the total GNP, yet they employed only 4.63 per cent of Taiwan's working labour force, and comprised 700–800 firms.[18] The business groups have heavily concentrated their investments and business operations in the capital- and technology-intensive industries, and they began to enter the financial sector in banking and securities after the state permitted new banks to be established in 1991. As in the 1980s, when the big industrial capitalists emerged in Taiwan's private business sector, a new breed of big financial capitalists will be formed by the mid-1990s. It is important to point out that behind these new private banks are, again, those powerful interests from the big industrial capitalists who merged their industrial capital into this newly opened financial sector. In other words, what will be seen is a rising joint economic force of the industrial and financial capitalists that will exert even more power and influence in the future political economic arena of Taiwan.

The Small and Medium Enterprises

Aside from the powerful state–party–private capital core are the large numbers of small and medium enterprises. In 1989, there were 773,511 registered business enterprises in Taiwan, 97.72 per cent of which were considered small and medium businesses, with turnover under NT$40 million (US$1.5 million) and total assets below NT$120 million (US$4.8 million). To make the picture more dramatic, 99 per cent of all enterprises in the manufacturing sector, for example food products, garments, non-metal furniture, and printing, were in the hands of these small and medium businessmen. They produced about 71 per cent of Taiwan's employment, and contributed 46.3 per cent of Taiwan's industrial production in value terms, yet they constituted only 26.11 per cent of all business sales.[19] According to the industrial and commercial surveys from 1966 to 1986, more than 95 per cent of all manufacturing units hired fewer than 50 employees, 80 per cent had fewer than 20, and 70 per cent fewer than ten.[20] However, the small and medium enterprises have been the backbone of Taiwan's trading economy, and accounted for more than 60 per cent of total exports in the 1980s. Taking only manufacturing exports alone, they contributed 65 per cent; and more than 70 per cent of the total business income of Taiwan's small and medium enterprises was generated from exports.

The above figures are an accurate depiction of Taiwan's small and medium business sector: they are not just relatively small compared to big businesses, they are small in absolute terms, in capital, sales, production, and labour employed in individual business units. Yet, as a whole, they provided far more jobs than big business did and they are the dynamism behind Taiwan's export economy, the number 12 trading power in the world in 1991. Moreover, the very existence of large numbers of small firms with significant capital decentralisation should be appreciated as one of the major structural reasons behind Taiwan's relatively equal income distribution at least before 1980. Obviously, the source of dynamism of small and medium business has been their links to the world market. Without this external market connection, the small and medium enterprises would not have been able to grow at such a rapid rate, from 170,000 in the early 1960s to more than 750,000 in the late 1980s. One of the key mechanisms provided by the state's EOI Policy to promote this dynamism was the tariff and tax rebate system. Under that policy, exporters were able to claim refunds on customs, duties and other taxes for the imports they required for export production. This policy mechanism has also helped to encourage Taiwan's exporters to be internationally competitive.

However, one could not conclude from this policy mechanism alone that small and medium enterprises were given special care by the state over the years. On the contrary, they have not been assisted financially in any other ways. In fact, they were left on their own to seek finance where they could. For decades, they were not able to take advantage of bank credit which went mainly to the state and private big enterprises. Only about 30 per cent of the loans from Taiwan's bank system have gone to the small and medium enterprises.[21] As a result, they were forced to be heavily dependent on the curbside or informal money market for their financial needs. The massive and widespread informal financial market, then, was critical to the survival and growth of Taiwan's small and medium enterprises, providing more than 80 per cent of their financial requirements in the early 1970s.[22] Even the small and medium enterprises still had to rely heavily on various informal and private financial sources such as rotating credit associations, which charged much higher interest rates than secured bank loans to which they were unable to get access. According to a report on the problems of Taiwan's small and medium enterprises, even in 1991 more than 40 per cent of this sector's financing still came from the private loan market.[23] Clearly, small and medium enterprises, in sharp contrast to big businesses, have been peripherised in the domestic political market *vis-à-vis* the state, even though they have been very active in their pursuit of material gains in the world economic market.

IV: THE CORPORATIST MECHANISMS OF STATE–BUSINESS RELATIONS

In order to make a broader and more penetrating analysis of state–business relations in post-war Taiwan, one should first identify the relations of the KMT state to the market. The concept of the 'governed market' as proposed by Wade in his criticism of neo-classical economic theorising in the East Asian formula of state and market relations is quite useful. Wade argues that East Asian economic performance has been due in large measure to a combination of (1) very high levels of productive investment making for rapid transfer to new techniques into actual production; (2) higher investment in certain key industries than would have occurred in the absence of government intervention; and (3) the exposure of many industries to international competition in foreign markets. In this formulation, the state, using incentives and controls, has been able to 'guide' and even 'govern' the market process of resource allocation so as to produce different production and investment outcomes.[24] The emphasis on dirigisme with the state directing or influencing the market, however, cannot be mistaken for a mere 'market repressing intervention'. As analysed elsewhere, the most important aspect of the dirigisme model is not that authoritarian political controls have made Taiwan's state intervention active and beneficial to development but that Taiwan has developed in spite of it.[25] Such a qualification on Taiwan's state versus market dynamics is crucial to the further understanding of the state–business relationship.

Partly due to its ideological inclination and partly to practical considerations, the KMT has established a material base for its political authoritarianism by its direct ownership of large state and party enterprises. The financial connections between government and the party establishment have always been an open secret. Its material endowments enabled the state to be in a more autonomous position *vis-à-vis* the private sector. Moreover, through its economic bureaucracy, the state enterprises and the party corporations, the state could effectively co-opt and integrate big business elites. Since the 1960s, the KMT state has been able to develop a coalition with the big private businesses, first of mainlanders and later of Taiwanese. The exchange of political loyalty and economic benefits and privileges has been the principle that has consolidated the state and big business.

Therefore, it is not surprising that almost all large private businesses and their founders in one way or another have strong ties to the state or the party.[26] Although these ties are not necessarily political, big businesses have all given their compliance to the authoritarian developmental state in order to maximise their profits primarily from a domestic market protected by state industrial policies, and that is why in the past four decades, under authoritarian KMT rule, no big business has ever challenged the state politically. As pointed out above, ethnic tension existed between the mainlander-controlled state and local Taiwanese-owned big business, but that simply gave Taiwanese capitalists another reason to be cautious about expressing any political opinion. They were perfectly aware that as long as they stayed neutral and understood the limits and did not challenge the state politically, they would be well taken care of by the equally sensitive state. This is not to suggest that the consensual relations between the state and big business were based on genuine trust and confidence. The assertion that the state has developed 'better' relations with business needs to be reconsidered in more political terms.[27] Rather, the tension between them and among businesses has been carefully managed to avoid conflict. In addition, though the state was responsible for protecting the market for big business, it was the state and party bureaucrats who decided who received privileges. Under such delicate conditions, personal connections and networks became crucial, and the cultivation of personal trust between business and political elites was a 'must' for individual businessmen.[28] Such personalised business–state relations further smoothed the potential tension that might have arisen from the overt political control exercised by the government. Again, the 1993 World Bank Report fails to see that such structural tensions long existed in business–government relations. Peng's study of the *guanxi* (relationships, connections, and networks) of Taiwan's big businessmen also found that the personal *guanxi* between the businessmen and the state elites and bureaucrats has been the base of the broadly defined political relations of the state with business. This was particularly evident among the first generation of big capitalists.[29] Nevertheless, the long lasting state–business relations are imbalanced, with the state in a pre-eminent position or, more accurately, the state has exercised 'paternalistic authority and dominance' over big business by which dirigisme was upheld and sustained until the recent political transition took place in the 1980s.[30]

One other important mechanism that has shaped the paternalistic authoritarian state–business relations has been the state corporatist control at all levels of business associations. Such a corporatist control mechanism was effectively and directly used by the party organs. As in many civil organisations, party organs from the central to local levels were responsible for supervision and surveillance. Within the private business sector, the national, provincial, and municipal trade associations were more or less administrative or even party arms of the KMT state. The KMT Central Headquarter's Department of Social Affairs has long possessed decisive power in determining the outcomes of elections to key positions of national business associations such as the National Federation of

Industries (NFI) and the National Federation of Commerce (NFC). Another cross-industrial, cross-sectoral body, the National Association of the Promotion of Industry and Commerce (NAPIC) was the same. NAPIC, organised in the 1950s, has been the forum for big business elites and the key state economic-financial officials who gather monthly for a breakfast meeting. As with the NFI and NFC, it functioned as a party political arm. Not coincidentally, since their establishment the chairmen of these three business associations have all been party members and some of them even have been awarded with posts in the Standing Committee of the KMT. The NFI and NFC were in the hands of the mainlander business elites prior to the 1970s, whereas NAPIC had Taiwanese business leaders in its governing body from the early 1960s. In a sense, NAPIC was considered to be a corporatist mechanism in which the KMT would integrate Taiwanese business elites into its political network.[31] Up until the late 1980s, the three national business organisations were all effective structures for the state's mobilisation of and control over Taiwan's big business sector. In addition, the taxation and intelligence branches of the government and party were bureaucratic arms used to keep business in check. This pattern of the state monitoring system of business was the same at provincial and local levels.

At the local level, state–business relations added another political dimension, the local political faction. The KMT has employed several mechanisms to co-opt or demobilise existing local factions that might threaten its rule at the local level.[32] The first mechanism was through arbitrary permission based on political consideration for specific factions to dominate certain local economic activities such as local bank branches, credit and cooperatives, producers' cooperatives, credit departments of the farmer and fishermen's associations, and local bus transportation. Among 89 county-based factions, 81 owned at least one of the above regional monopoly activities. The second tool the state used was through privileged loans granted by public banks. Almost all provincial assemblymen could gain access to such a privilege with the state party's permission. The third was through granting contracts for public works at the local level, a tool by which local factions could maximise their gains. The fourth means was to benefit particular factions with windfall profits under the guise of legal or administrative procedures such as city planning or public infrastructure projects. Many land speculation schemes were, in fact, means by which the local factions and political entrepreneurs could engage with the local or central party state bureaucracy. In some cases nominally illegal economic activities such as illicit gambling, dancing and prostitution were protected by the local government and party.

One of the political consequences is that those local factions and political entrepreneurs grew bigger and stronger under the state's patronage and even became a direct threat to the state's legitimate rule if they sought price increases. Toward the end of the 1980s, the growing tension between the state and the local factions and the local economic interests became a constant problem for the party which ended up having to negotiate and compromise at every election. In other words the clientelism that the KMT has relied on to deepen its domination of local politics through the distribution of economic rewards has been challenged by the powerful local political entrepreneurs at the same time as authoritarianism at the central level was undergoing a transition to democracy. However, the tension was more often driven by the ambition of the local factions to move upward to the national political arena than by notions of democracy.

What happened to those small and medium enterprises which have been, in most part, excluded from the political economic interests bloc that protected the domestic market for big business and local political factions? As discussed previously, they turned to the foreign markets to find economic opportunity and a share in the prosperity of the world economy. State policy did provide incentives for boosting exports, but did not offer a deliberately favourable political environment for any particular enterprise to receive special privileges as it did to big business. The state also did not develop any sophisticated mechanism to integrate the small and medium business sector into its corporatist structure. Furthermore, small export businesses have not been assisted by the state and public banking system when they needed financial assistance, and the risks they took in entering the unknown world market were taken on their own. Without state support or political favours, the small and medium businessmen turned to the traditional networks of their families and friends for help. The family enterprises which make up the bulk of the small and medium business sector, though dynamic and flexible in their response to the changing world market situations, have been limited in growth and expansion by the hands-off attitude of the state. The success of small and medium enterprises in foreign markets has been very impressive but it should not be misconceived as proof of the state's 'perspicacious' free market policy. As noted above, the state is by no means a free market follower in its governing of Taiwan's domestic market. Hamilton, however, has praised Taiwan's state–business relations as a 'strong society model' where the state has '[let] the people prosper'.[33] But such assertion should be reassessed.

First, under the KMT government's authoritarian corporatism, civil society in general and the business community in particular has never been strong *vis-à-vis* the state. Nor do the dynamic small and medium enterprises, which developed into a 'strong' private sector and were relatively free from the state's heavy control, support Hamilton's assertion as the strength of this sector was an unintended result. Furthermore, in the course of export development the small and medium enterprises were in no position to be termed 'strong' *vis-à-vis* the state bureaucracy. Second, the KMT state will let business prosper only if business resumes political loyalty for economic gain, as is quite evident in the case of big business. As for small business, the state has let it prosper with the world rather than the domestic market, which the state has protected for its big business clients. Thus Hamilton's 'letting small business prosper' in the foreign markets has happened only by default because the state has been preoccupied politically with the domestic market. It merely opened a door for politically weak small business to compete in the risk-ridden world economy. To be sure, large numbers of small and medium enterprises have prospered and have created the Taiwan miracle, but this can by no means be attributed to a genuinely pro-small business ideology or strategy on the part of the state.

The most striking aspect of state–small business relations is the relative lack of political calculation in the interaction when compared to state–big business relations. The contacts of small export manufacturers with the state were much more on the bureaucratic than the political level, so they actually have a very loose and indirect relation with the state itself. In the eyes of the KMT state, the scattered small-scale businesses oriented to economic opportunities outside of Taiwan constitute very little if any threat to the regime. Therefore, the state has not paid attention to business associations representing them. Lacking state political connections, the small and medium enterprises, in order for their businesses to survive and develop, turned to the other two networks to get the necessary resources, the kin networks and other affective ties expressed in *guanxi* relationships, that of classmate, co-worker, same provincial origin, same local origin, same surname, and so on. The other kind is the marketing links forged with foreign corporations. The OEM arrangement, based on subcontracting at the level of local production units, has been the most common link with the world markets, through US buyers such as K Mart, Sears, J.C. Penny, Hewlett-Packard, Texas Instruments, and IBM, and the Japanese multinational enterprises. Actually it is the Japanese marketing firms which have played the more crucial role in arranging and controlling Taiwan's exports, handling an estimated one-third to 50 per cent of the trade. The major Japanese trading firms that have operated in Taiwan include Mitsubishi, Marubeni, Mitsui, and Beisei.[34] In other words, behind a glorified picture of the dynamic small and medium export sector is this reality characterised by its marginalised political role, unsupported by state credit policy, racked by the self-perpetuation of traditional business practices, and its dependence on the high-interest informal money market.

V: THE CHANGES AND THE FUTURE PROSPECTS OF STATE–BUSINESS RELATIONS

After almost three decades of authoritarian yet corporatist state–big business relations, the common interests of the two political economic sectors in Taiwan have consolidated and deepened their relationships. Behind these relations is the growing influence of big business interests on the state's decision making process through direct and indirect means. This has been becoming more evident since the 1980s, when both political liberalisation and organised social movements began to take shape. It should be added that increasing pressures from big business on the state would realise anyway as more people benefited from the spread effect of the cumulative capital. However, as state authoritarianism became increasingly pressured by the demands of the political democratisation originating from society at large, the growing political influences of big business became more and more visible.[35] The most noticeable indication of direct business participation in Taiwan politics can be found in the growing involvement in national elections of the capitalist class, beginning in the 1980s. The increasing number of seats held by business elites in Taiwan's law-making body, the Legislative Yuan, has been most significant. As Kuo has demonstrated, based on the composition of the class origins of the candidates and the elected Legislative members from 1972 to 1989, the capitalist class has occupied more and more seats over the past two-decade period, in sharp contrast to the working class and the middle classes. Though the percentages of candidates who are managers and company presidents were stable (21–25 per cent), the percentage of those elected increased noticeably from 19.4 per cent in 1972 to 30.6 per cent in 1989. Kuo's study further shows that, if one groups bosses, proprietors and other big businessmen together as the 'capitalist class', then more than 45 per cent of the 1989 Legislative Yuan members represented the capitalists' interests. Moreover, there is a great increase in the number of commercial and financial capitalists holding seats in this body, while that of the manufacturing industrialists remained the same. As discussed above, the empowerment of the Taiwanese business class is also reflected in the changing ethnic composition of the Legislative Yuan since 1980. Finally, the KMT was much more inclined to endorse capitalist and big businessmen as party candidates for various elected posts since the 1980s, as the money factor has increasingly become crucial in elections.[36]

Moving from the central to the local level of the political arena, according to Chen's analysis of the class background of provincial assemblymen between 1968 and 1985, capitalists and top executives from both private and public enterprises held as many as 75 per cent of all the seats. This further demonstrates the over-representation of this class interest in the law-making process.[37] This observation is also supported by an analysis of the occupational backgrounds of provincial, county, and township councilmen who were elected in the 1970s and 1980s.[38] Thus, it is quite evident that under the authoritarian paternalistic state, Taiwan's business class, especially from big business, has been nurtured in great number and has gradually been moved into all levels of politics. Big businessmen have concentrated their political influence at the central level, while the local factions with strong business–economic links control the local levels. Meanwhile the large number of small and medium entrepreneurs have, over the years, been virtually excluded from the political process at the central level, though some have involved themselves in local politics. But compared to their big business counterparts they are at the political periphery.

With their more visible and stronger representations at the central political level, big business interests have increased the protection they enjoy, and their interests have been promoted at the expense of other social and public groups. Since the 1980s, a number of industrial and financial policies and laws were made to favour big business interests, while some checking proposals were blocked or deferred. Some examples favouring business interests include: the 1984 Ministry of Economic Affairs' proposed policy change in the textile exports code which was first resisted then later greatly modified so as to protect the vested interests of the big textile magnates; the 1989 Ministry of Finance decision to re-collect the tax on stock exchange profits received a strong setback by those legislative members with interests in the stock exchange; and finally the Ministry had to reduce the tax rate from the originally planned 1.5 per cent to only 0.6 per cent in order not to upset the financiers.[39]

Protection of business is seen in cases such as the strong resistance of capitalist interests in the Legislative Yuan to the government's decision to enact the Consumer Protection Law, the Environmental Protection Law, the Fair Trade Law, and the Environmental Impact Assessment Act. Though the Fair Trade Law and the Consumer Protection Law were finally passed in 1991 and 1993 respectively after a more than ten-year delay in the Legislative Yuan, the other two are still pending as they are perceived by many capitalist legislators to threaten business interests. Big business interest groups still take a wait and see attitude toward the now enacted Fair Trade Law and the Consumer Protection Law. The social and economic objectives of these two laws are to regulate big business practices and to avoid or minimise the social inequality caused by the expansion of the business conglomerates. However, according to the big business elites, it is the state companies and party enterprises with heavy state protection and special privileges which should first be vigorously regulated. In other words, a certain degree of resentment is shared by the business elites towards the state's 'anti-business' sentiment revealed in these laws. However, such negative attitudes are not shared by the larger non-business population. What one has seen is a state seemingly too weak to make autonomous policy decisions when confronted with big business interests. Not only is the Legislative Yuan increasingly controlled by capitalist members but also these interests dominate the crucial Economic and Finance Committees of this body.

The liberalisation of the authoritarian KMT state as demanded by the political opposition and by popular social movements since the 1980s has already transformed the state from a hard authoritarianism to a soft authoritarianism.[40] In the process of adjustment, existing functions of the state bureaucracy and the old rules of the game are no longer useful in governing society at large. As the government adjusts itself to be more responsive rather than domineering in facing various and often conflicting demands from civil society, the powerful interest groups have often taken advantage of what appears to be a 'puzzled' state. To put it more critically, it was the non-business sector of civil society and the political opposition that have forced the authoritarian KMT to liberalise,[41] yet it is the big business annd capitalist interests which have benefited most financially from this political liberalisation. Big business was protected in the domestic market during the authoritarian phase, and now, during the liberalising and democratising phase, it is able to exploit the situation to either minimise its losses or maximise its possible gains.

But the small and medium enterprises have not been so fortunate in the course of political transformation. In the 1980s, the export manu- facturers have faced many internal developmental problems such as a labour shortage, rising labour costs, and escalating land prices. They also experienced external threats from Southeast Asian manufacturers, protectionism from the West, and since the mid-1980s they have seen their competitiveness in world markets further reduced by the appreciation of the Taiwan dollar. The official policies adopted by the state to deal with development problems have included industrial restructuring from labour- intensive to capital-intensive and high-tech industries, diversification of export trade, and the transferring of labour-intensive industries from Taiwan to the Southeast Asian region. However, these policies have not solved the immediate and desperate short-run problems that the small export producers and traders have faced. To small firms, the above state policies were at best a long-term solution to Taiwan's industrial develop- ment; they were not a workable and effective remedy for their immediate survival. Thus, through the bad times of the 1980s, they have had, once again, to rely on their own efforts to survive. As in the 1960s and the 1970s, they took risks in the foreign export markets, exploring the labour market in Southeast Asia and mainland China in order to transfer or expand their operations there. In Southeast Asia, it is the traditional Chinese networks, not state assistance, that has produced their business opportunities. In mainland China, as direct trade and investment were legally prohibited until 1990, they risked punishment by the KMT state. They were the first group to engage in 'unofficial' economic relations with the mainland. Their self-made spirit, quick response to new opportunities, and willingness to risk what they had once again helped them to succeed.

In the late 1980s and the early 1990s, the KMT state reluctantly endorsed a series of more open policies toward Taiwan's trade and investment with mainland China. The state finally recognised the reality of active Taiwanese trade and investment on the mainland. The Mainland Affair Council at the central government was established and a semi-governmental Straits Exchange Foundation was formed. Together they are responsible for future policy-making and implementation at official and unofficial levels. The Straits Foundation is charged by the KMT with a mission of 'front line' contact with PRC officials in dealing with civilian and business disputes. In retrospect, behind the changed mainland policy was, in large part, the initiatives and pressures of the big capitalists.[42] It was only after big business entered into mainland investment and developed vested interests there and only after it began to exert pressures on the state through various channels that the state shifted its mainland policies to more pragmatic ones. President Lee Teng-Hui, unlike the late Chiang Chin-Kuo and his father Chiang Kai-Shek who held an anti-capitalist business ideology, is known for his favourable attitudes toward business, and he has a number of close Taiwanese big business friends. During the power transition when faction struggles were occurring, President Lee even asked the most influential Taiwanese capitalists to act as mediators. He often consults with them on economic issues, and trade and investment policies on mainland China were certainly the main concerns at this time.[43] Besides this direct influence on the president from big business interests, the Legislative Yuan was also a source of pressure on state officials through those elected capitalist members demanding more liberal and open trade policies towards the PRC. The close relationship between the KMT and big business on the mainland issue was also revealed by the fact that many influential capitalists are donors to the Straits Exchange Foundation and serve as board members.

The small and medium enterprises initially took political risks to open the mainland market and demonstrated the profitability of that market to big business; and later big business followed with greater financial and political power. Under the more flexible mainland policies, though the small manufacturers have also benefited, they now have to face competition from their fellow big businessmen on the mainland for labour and raw materials; they also worry that their existing privileges to do business on the mainland by informal means may disappear once the communication and formal relations between the two sides are officially institutionalised, as is actively promoted by big business interests. One should not, however, evaluate the overall impact of Taiwan's political transition from authoritarianism as based only on its repercussions on state–business relations. The weakening autonomy of the state's economic and social policy making in the face of strong and organised pressure from big business interests caused alarm. Many concerned critics feel that the transformation favouring business at the expense of the general public interest was the crucial factor in the worsening of social inequality in Taiwan through the 1980s. This is not to suggest that the pre-liberalisation state–business relationship was better, but merely points to the fact that the state is being trapped in a political economic setting of its own making with the costs incurred transferred to society as a whole. The state, in its attempts to bring big business back into a patron–client relationship, has not only acceded in various policies to big business interests but has also engaged in a number of aggressive actions to win back business political loyalty and support.

First, ever since General Hau Pei-tsun took power as Premier in mid-1990 as a compromise candidate resulting from the intra-party struggle between reform and conservative factions and between Taiwanese and mainlander ethnic lines, the state began to take tougher positions in response to the demands of the labour and environmental movements, both of which threatened business interests. The criminal code was applied to suppress the activism by a civil society mobilised in the form of organised social protests. Second, in order to win the confidence of business, the state insisted on going ahead with the controversial industrial projects that had been effectively halted for some years by opposed environmental groups and local residents. Typical examples are the questionable industrial zone in central Taiwan, China Petroleum's construction of the fifth Naphtha Cracking Refinery in the south before it had solved the serious pollution problems already affecting the local community, Formosa Plastics' new petrochemical refinery in the south-west coastal area, and the hotly debated fourth nuclear power plant to be constructed by the Taiwan Power Company in northern Taiwan. All these actions were aimed at strengthening state power and developing a new coalition with big business. Third, in mid-1991, the ambitious Six Year National Construction Plan was launched by the Premier with a total budget of NT$8.2 trillion (about US$310 billion) with the dual political economic purpose of strengthening Taiwan's links with foreign capital and further tightening state–business connections through the sharing of this newly created economic pie. Fourth, in a more directly political move, the state party began to forge a new coalition with the up and coming business elites, those destined to be the successors to well-established big businesses. A fourth cross-sectoral business group was formed in the Council of Industrial and Commerical Development (CICD). Its members are hand-picked participants in a KMT-sponsored business leaders training programme. The CICD can be seen as a rival to the established NFI, NFC, and NAPIC which are controlled by the older generation of business leaders, competing for political favours and influences. Since the CICD has a large number of successful medium sized exporters as members, it can also be seen as a move to cultivate a domestic political market that has long been dominated by big business.

The state party, on the other hand, sees it as a check on the overly powerful big business interests. It is therefore important to see how the CICD will interact with the state power and how it will affect changing state–business relations. Fifth, besides developing an alliance with the new business elites, the state has also tried to restrengthen its political control over all business by expressing its disapproval towards some businessmen's support for the opposition Democratic Progressive Party (DPP) and their activities. In a speech to a group of important business leaders in September 1991, ex-Premier Hau warned his business audience in a rather coercive tone not to support the DPP-backed Taiwan Independence movement. Though such an overtly political statement was later severely criticised by the DPP and the public, the intention behind it cannot be ignored.

So far, the increasing political influence of big business backed by its accumulation of capital during the course of political transition from authoritarianism to democracy might have also further weakened the KMT state's relative autonomy *vis-à-vis* civil society. But the state, in responding to such an unprecedented challenge, has shown its bias toward big business by conceding to its interests on the one hand, and repressing the demands for social and economic reforms expressed in popular social movements on the other. It may be unfair to say that the liberalising state has maintained its control over civil society. By lifting various bans on civil organisations, the press, and specific religious organisations, the state did respond to the demands of liberalisation from society and has tried to be more responsive to the needs of various segments of the general public. However, what is at issue here is not the mere softening of the tight control on society, but whether or not the state has redirected the sources for its political legitimacy to broader and more democratic bases. Essentially, the transition to democracy requires a reorganisation of the overall state–society relationship in a more balanced and egalitarian direction.

The liberalisation of the authoritarian KMT state was exploited by business to expand its political and economic interests, even at the expense of general well-being and social justice. New state–society relationships have not yet been institutionalised, and unfortunately the state has not shown any sign of a definite move in this direction. It has instead taken a different tack, narrowing its political base to the capitalist sector by reinforcing its ties with established big business and extending this coalition to include the newly emerged business elites from the export sector. Social movements, despite their primary objectives of political liberalisation, more equality and economic justice have the potential to prevent the weakened state from falling further into the hands of the increasingly powerful big business sector.[44] In other words, the social movements may not only press the state to loosen its control over society but also demand that it redirects its class and sectoral coalitions. The state could develop a coalition with the forces behind the social movements and reshape its imbalanced relations with big business interests. The crucial task before the KMT state at present is to apprehend immediately the new reality. To accept the irreversible trend towards democracy should be the starting point of the reformers in the political centre to generate popular support and accelerate further democratisation. As for future state–civil society relations, the state should recognise the new social interest groups emerging in the various social movements. Recognising the new elements and social forces in various sectors of the civil society is to accommodate the demands for social movements and to actively engage in a social transition from 'authoritarian corporatism' to 'democratic corporatism'. In such a model of state–civil society relations, the state does not assume unified direction and control, but can assume a more autonomous position, not beholden to any particular class or powerful interest group.

NOTES

1. H.-H.M. Hsiao, 'Development Strategies and Class Transformation in Taiwan and South Korea: Origins and Consequences', *Bulletin of the Institute of Ethnology, Academia Sinica*, Vol.61 (1987), pp.183–217; B.-L. Lee, *State and Socio-economic Development in Taiwan* (Temple University Ph.D., 1991); C.-K. Pang, *The State and Economic Transformation: the Taiwan Case* (New York, 1992).
2. World Bank, *The East Asian Miracle: Economic Growth and Public Policy* (Oxford, 1993).
3. T.-C. Chou, 'The Small and Medium Enterprises in Power Periphery', in H.-H.M. Hsiao *et al.* (eds.), *Monopoly and Exploitation: The Political Economy of Authoritarianism* (in Chinese) (Taipei, 1989).
4. H.-H.M. Hsiao, 'The Farmer's Movement in Taiwan in the 1980s: Fact and Explanations' (in Chinese), *Bulletin of the Institute of Ethnology, Academia Sinica*, Vol.70 (1991), pp.67–94.
5. R. Wade, *Governing the Market: Economic Theory and the Role of Government in East Asian Industrialisation* (Princeton, 1990).
6. W. Bello, 'The Spread and Impact of Export-Orientated Industrialisation in the Pacific-Rim', *Third World Economics* (1991).
7. Ibid.
8. G.-S. Shieh, 'Black-hands Becoming Their Own Bosses: Class Mobility in Taiwan's Manufacturing Sectors' (in Chinese), *Taiwan: A Radical Quarterly in Social Studies*, Vol.2 (1989), pp.11–54.
9. See Lee, *State and Socio-economic Development*.
10. See A. Amsden, 'Taiwan's Economic History', *Modern China*, Vol.5 (1979), pp.341–79; 'The State and Taiwan's Economic Development', in P. Evans *et al.* (eds.), *Bringing the State Back* (Cambridge, 1985); L.-W. Kuo, 'Capital Formation and Social Inequality in Taiwan' (UCLA Ph.D., 1991); S.M. Chen *et al.*, *Disintegrating KMT–State Capitalism* (in Chinese) (Taipei, 1991).
11. B.-H. Lee, 'The Debate on Taiwan's Public Enterprises and State Capitalism' (in Chinese), Conference on 'The State and Society in Democratizing Taiwan', March 1992.
12. Chen *et al.*, *Disintegrating KMT–State Capitalism*.
13. Y.-H. Chu, 'Monopolistic Economy and Authoritarian Political System', in Hsiao *et al.* (eds.), *Monopoly and Exploitation*, pp.115–38.
14. *Asian Wall Street Journal Weekly*, 9 Oct. 1989.

15. H.-C. Peng, 'The Guanxi and its Transformation of Taiwan's Entrepreneurs' (in Chinese) (Tunghai University Ph.D., 1989).
16. W. Bello and S. Rosenfeld, *Dragons in Distress: Asia's Miracle Economics in Crisis* (San Francisco, 1990).
17. I. Namazaki, 'Networks of Taiwanese Big Business: A Preliminary Analysis', *Modern China*, Vol.12 (1986).
18. China Credit Institute 1990–91.
19. C.-L. Wei, 'The Business–State Relationship and its Development of Taiwan's Big and Small-Medium Enterprises', in *Proceedings of the Conference on the Relations of Business, Government and Society* (in Chinese) (Taipei, 1991).
20. Shieh, 'Black-hands Becoming Their Own Bosses'.
21. C.-C. Lin, 'The Mutual Exploitation Cycle of the Underprivileged Groups under Authoritarianism', in Hsiao *et al.* (eds.), *Monopoly and Exploitation*, pp.161–96.
22. Bello and Rosenfeld, *Dragons in Distress*.
23. *China Time Evening Post*, 5 April 1992.
24. Wade, *Governing the Market*.
25. H.-H.M. Hsiao, 'Explaining the Taiwan Development Model: Lessons to be Learnt', in D. Kim *et al.*, *The Role of the Market and State: Economic and Social Reforms in East Asia and East-Central Europe* (Seoul, 1992) pp.127–47.
26. H.-H.M. Hsiao, 'The Entrepreneurial Process of Taiwan's Small-Medium and Big Businessmen' (in Chinese), *Journal of Chinese Sociology*, Vol.16 (1992), pp.139–68.
27. See World Bank, *East Asian Miracle*.
28. See Hsiao, 'Entrepreneurial Process'.
29. See Peng, 'The Guanxi'.
30. See C.-M. Chang, 'Business–Government Relations in Post-War Taiwan', *Journal of Sinology: A Social Science Quarterly*, Vol.6 (1991), pp.13–34.
31. R.-H. Hsu, 'Trade Associations under State Corporatism', Paper presented at Conference on 'History and Culture in Modern China', Academia Sinica, Taipei, June 1991.
32. Chu, 'Monopolistic Economy'.
33. G. Hamilton and N.W. Biggart, 'Market Culture and Authority: A Comparative Analysis of Management and Organisation in the Far East', *American Journal of Sociology*, Vol.94 (1988), pp.52–94.
34. Bello and Rosenfeld, *Dragons in Distress*; Lin, 'Mutual Exploitation Cycle'.
35. H.-H.M. Hsiao, 'The Rise of Social Movements and Civil Protests', in T.J. Cheng *et al.* (eds.), *Political Change in Taiwan* (1992), pp.57–72.
36. Kuo, 'Capital Formation and Social Inequality'.
37. M.-T. Chen, 'The Mobility of Local Political Elites under an Authoritarian Regime, 1945–1986' (in Chinese) (National University of Taiwan Ph.D., 1990).
38. Chen *et al.*, *Disintigrating KMT–State Capitalism*.
39. Kuo, 'Capital Formation and Social Inequality'.
40. See E. Winckler, 'Taiwan Transition?', in *Political Change in Taiwan* (1992), pp.221–59.
41. See Hsiao, 'Farmer's Movement in Taiwan', 'Rise of Social Movements', and 'Labor Movement in Taiwan: Retrospects and Prospects', in D.F. Simon *et al.* (eds.), *Beyond the Economic Miracle* (New York, 1992), pp.151–67.
42. H.-H.M. Hsiao and A. So, 'Ascent Through National Integration: the Chinese Triangle of Mainland-Taiwan-Hong Kong', in R. Palat (ed.), *Asia-Pacific and the Future of the World Economy* (Connecticut, 1993) pp.133–47.
43. T.-C. Su, *Power and Money* (in Chinese) (Taipei, 1992).
44. See Hsiao, 'Farmer's Movement in Taiwan', 'Rise of Social Movements', and 'Labor Movement in Taiwan'.

Changing Business–Government Relations in Korea

KU-HYUN JUNG

South Korean society has transformed itself from an agrarian society to an industrial one in a short 30-year period between 1960 and 1990. A recent census result shows that in 1990 74.4 per cent of the Korean people lived in urban areas. Thirty years ago, 80 per cent of the Korean people lived in rural areas. Other demographic statistics show that Korean society is rapidly approaching an industrial society. Life expectancy has almost caught up with that of major industrialised countries, and the birth rate has declined to 1.6 children per couple. Per capita income reached the level of over US$6,000 in 1991, but some selected areas of Seoul demonstrate a much higher consumption level. Table 1 shows some indicators of the quality of life in three East Asian economies. Several factors characterise the rapid industralisation and economic growth of Korea in the last 30 years. The initial condition was the war-destroyed economy subsisting on American aid, but with a relatively good supply of educated and skilled people. An authoritarian leader with a strong desire for national modernisation emerged and began to oversee the industriali-sation process in the next two decades. Beginning in the early 1970s, exporting was given the highest priority by the government and has been subsidised heavily. Domestic industries were protected from foreign competition during the 1960s and 1970s, and the labour movement has been suppressed by the state. Government funds as well as bank loans have been channelled to a small number of successful companies, and the latter were often heavily protected even from domestic competition by government regulation. This set of policies has brought about an economy that is characterised by strong, interventionist government and a group of very powerful private business firms called *chaebol*.

The democratisation process which symbolically started around 1987 has challenged the fundamental structure of the Korean economy and society that had been formulated during the previous three developmental decades. The purpose of this paper is to argue that traditional business–government relations are not adequate for Korea to compete in the increasingly competitive global environment. In fact, it will be argued that heavy government intervention and close business–government relations are major obstacles that will retard the quality upgrading of the Korean economy in the 1990s and beyond. Before looking at

Ku-Hyun Jung, Yonsei University

TABLE 1

QUALITY OF LIFE: KOREA, TAIWAN AND JAPAN (1990)

	Korea	Taiwan	Japan
Income:			
GNP per capita (US$)	5,569.0	7,954.0	23,968.0
Unemployment rate (%)	2.4	1.7	2.1
Gini coefficient	0.335	0.303	0.268
	(1988)	(1989)	(1988)
Environment:			
Water pollution/BOD (mg/l)	2.0		2.5
Air pollution (ppm) (SO2)	0.036	0.026	0.010
Industrial waste (kg per capita)	515.0		2579.0
Dwelling space (m sq per capita)	13.8	28.1	25.2
Welfare:			
Traffic accidents (deaths per 1000)	28.8	19.2	9.0
			(1989)
Road availability (m per car)	16.7	6.8	20.1
			(1989)
Violent offences (murder, robbery, rape) (cases per 1000)	25.0	34.0	5.0
Life expectancy (years)	71.0	74.0	79.0
Social security expenditure (% of government expenditure)	9.4	17.3	17.5

Sources: National Statistical Office, *Social Indicators in Korea* (1991); Directorate-General of Budgets, Accounting and Statistics, *Social Indicators in Taiwan Area of the Republic of China* (1990); Government Administration Bureau of Statistics, *Statistical Year-Book in Japan* (1991).

business–government relations, it is necessary to look at a cultural characteristic that underlies the unique business–government relations in Korea.

I: *KWAN-KEI* CULTURE

One driving-force in Korean society is personal relationships or connections. Primary groups such as family, school ties or geographical ties are the bonds which maintain small networks of personal relationships. This phenomenon is not unique to Korean society but is also found in Japan or China. It is called *guansi* in Chinese, *kankei* in Japanese and *kwan-kei* in

Korean. Since primary group ties cross over institutional affiliations, business and government relations are really translated into personal relationships between government officials and business managers at individual levels. For example, political parties in Korea are still very much followings of particular individuals rather than groupings of ideological belief. Loyalty to individuals is more important than any abstract ideology or betterment of social welfare. Likewise, personal relationships are more important than some objective criterion in governmental and business decisions. One can argue that this kind of relationship-oriented culture is a characteristic of a traditional, even tribal, society. As the society becomes an industrial one, this kind of social characteristic may change. Since Korea has achieved the status of an industrial society in such a short period of time, it is possible that the remnants of an agricultural society still linger on.

It is not necessary for this paper to determine whether the primary group oriented behaviour of Korean society is due to cultural characteristics or to a particular stage of social development. The point is that current Korean society is very much characterised by strong attachments to primary groups and we have to take this into account in order to understand contemporary Korean society. Primary group relationships cross over the boundaries of secondary organisations. This means that in business–government relations primary group ties allow the executives in business to be close to government officials. In other words, business executives will constantly try to court government officials for personal relationships. This kind of relationship would bring about charges of nepotism in a Western culture but may be accepted as a social norm in Korean society. In addition, the fact that decision-making is concentrated in one city, Seoul, makes the *kwan-kei* culture more visible. Since Seoul accounts for more than 60 per cent of economic power in the nation and most influential people live in the city, special ties between business executives and high government officials are maintained through frequent informal meetings. Moreover, the relatively small role that the foreign business community plays in the Korean economy makes domestic business and government circles very homogeneous and closely knit.

II: GOVERNMENT INTERVENTION AND ITS FAILURES

There is a misconception about the Korean economy among some Western economists when they describe it as a model of free market enterprise. Korea has never experienced an extensive free market economy. The market would have had only a limited function during the agrarian Korean society which prevailed until the nineteenth century. The Japanese colonial government pursued a heavily interventionist policy in exploiting the Korean people. The Rhee regime had the best example of a market economy between 1953 and 1960, but the economy during that period lacked productive activities which could drive the market. During the developmental decades beginning in the early 1960s, the government again turned heavily interventionist. The current business–government relationship in Korea is a product of the interaction between the two sectors during the last 30 years.[1]

The traditional role of the Korean government in the economy could be described as in Table 2. Many of the targeted industries in the so-called heavy and chemical sector reveal economies of scale. As a result, the government had a licensing system whereby it allowed only a small number of companies to enter an industry and prevented other firms from doing so. The state also channelled money to a targeted industry by allocating its own funds and by directing commercial banks under the direct control of the government. These funds were made available to private firms in the form of loans. Therefore, the ultimate responsibility for utilising and paying back those loans was placed in the hands of private business firms. When private companies with heavy government borrowings became insolvent due to mismanagement, the government or a bank will be directly involved in finding a new company which can take over the insolvent one together with the debt.

It can be seen from the above discussion that resource allocation and entry–exit regulation by the government are closely linked. Since the government has been directly involved from the initial stage of industry development to the mature stage, it is natural for government bureaucrats to feel that they are guiding and supervising the industry. Even today it is possible to read in Korean newspapers of the Ministry of Trade and Industry announcing specific production and export targets not only for an industry but also for particular companies in the industry. This may seem very strange to an observer from a Western market economy. In any case, the Korean way of developing a certain target industry through the

TABLE 2

TRADITIONAL GOVERNMENTAL ROLE IN THE KOREAN ECONOMY

High Activity	Low Activity
Resource Allocation	Income Distribution
Entry and Exit Regulation	Social Welfare
Direct Ownership of Enterprises	Anti-Trust Regulation
Price and Wage Controls	Pollution Control

cooperation of the government and business is neither a free market economy nor a centrally planned economy. It is a regulated market economy. The question is whether a regulated market economy has been efficient compared to the alternatives. This is a difficult question to answer. Theoretical literature on the subject deals with incidents of market or government failure. But the Korean case is a mixture of the market and government, and the theories dealing with pure markets and pure governments are of limited value here.[2] It seems clear that a regulated market economy is superior to a centrally planned economy. But is a regulated market economy more efficient than a free market economy?

The answer to the preceding question seems to be affirmative at the early stage of industrialisation when there are not enough resources for industry development. All the ingredients for successful industry development are lacking: technology, capital, management, human resources and even raw materials. The government mobilises the resources inside and outside the country and channels them to successful and trustworthy entrepreneurs. The latter, in turn, work hard in order to make profits and build their own empires.[3] Under these circumstances, government regulation of an industry has two major potential problems: misjudging the demand either way and/or inefficient operation of the enterprise due to the lack of competition. Several factors may have worked to prevent these problems from occurring in the Korean context. First, at the early stage of industrialisation, the supply tends to create its own demand, and the shortage of resources tends to limit the size of a plant to the minimum economic scale. There are exceptions to this when a particular government is more interested in protecting an industry rather than its efficiency. In the Korean case, since private companies were eventually responsible for making the venture profitable, they may have been keen to avoid over-capacity. Lack of domestic competition and the resulting inefficiency have been partially compensated by foreign competition overseas. In the export industries, international competition forced private companies to be efficient in order to survive.

As the economy moved to a more mature stage toward the end of the 1970s, the regulated market economy started to reveal some failures. The over-capacity and under-utilisaton of plant became serious problems in some heavy industries, especially defence-related industries. The lack of competition in some industries may have made management rather lax and inefficient. As the domestic economy began to be open to foreign competition, these inefficient industries suddenly became vulnerable. There have been several cases of government failures since the late 1970s. First and foremost would be excessive investment in the heavy machinery industry, notably its defence sector. Overcapacity and the resulting losses have persisted in the Korea Heavy Industries Corporation. Secondly, there was a case of the shipping industry. The government provided various incentives to private firms in order to increase the total capacity of the national flag carriers, and the companies who followed government policy found themselves later in serious financial troubles. Eventually, the industry as a whole had to go through a major reorganisation when many companies became bankrupt. Another case would be the restructuring of the automotive industry in the early 1980s. Because of the recession, the domestic automotive industry ran into serious problems because of overcapacity and mounting losses. The government intervened to restructure the industry, forcing companies to become specialised in the production of passenger cars and trucks or buses. In retrospect, one can question the efficacy of the restructuring policy. Non-intervention may have resulted in a better long-term performance by eliminating inefficient competitors from the industry.

The over-regulation of industry still persists. Despite the announced policy of liberalising entry into major industries, the government is still involved. Taking again the case of the automobile industry, the government has recently blocked some companies from entering. There are strong reasons for government intervention and there are many who argue for it. They believe that if free entry is allowed this will result in excessive investment and cut-throat competition. The waste of 'national resources' will follow. The automobile industry has many natural entry barriers such as large production plant, technology, and the presence of loyal suppliers and a distribution channel. These natural entry barriers are more than enough to prevent many potential entrants. Government regulation is a redundant barrier which hinders effective competition in the industry. If there are some companies seeking to enter the industry, this may be an indication that either the current competitors are not very efficient or potential entrants are miscalculating the industry's potential. The issue is one of who is in a better position to forecast the future potential of the automobile industry, the government or a private business firm. It is also possible that a new entrant might possess new technology which the existing companies either do not have or are reluctant to utilise due to their already committed position. It is worth pointing out that a breakthrough innovation is sometimes introduced from outside the industry. Quartz technology for the watch industry is an example. It is possible that an industry could suffer from over-capacity and excessive competition after free entry is allowed. The choice is between freer competition with the possibility of over-investment or a regulated industry with the possibility of inefficiency and under-innovation. The choice is not between a perfect market and a perfect government, but between an imperfect market and an imperfect government. As the economy becomes more mature, an imperfect market tends to perform better than an imperfect government. First, there are not as many new industries as in the early industrialisation stage when the country has to mobilise limited resources to build new industries. As a result, the waste of resources argument is less convincing. Secondly, private companies would have gained enough experience to exercise their own judgement about an industry and enough resources to enter a new industry. Thirdly, in the age of global competition, only companies that have been seasoned in fierce domestic competition can survive in the global market. In addition, when a government has to allow foreign competitors into the domestic market, how can it not allow domestic companies to enter a certain industry?

A stronger argument for government failure can be made about the direct ownership of key enterprises by the government. There are dozens of state-owned enterprises in Korea and many of them operate in the monopolistic market. Some of them are very large even compared to the private big business groups. Since many of these state enterprises also operate in highly regulated industries, their profits do not represent the performance of the companies. As a result, these companies are not operating like business firms but more like government offices. In many cases, retired high government officials or generals are appointed to the top posts of these state companies. In state enterprises, there is little sense of the 'urgency' that is often found in private companies and little incentive to innovate. The situation is not very different from the state enterprises in socialist countries.

All in all, the Korean government should change its role in the coming decade. It has to dramatically reduce its activity in areas where it has been previously instrumental. They are the areas of direct fund allocation, entry and exit barriers, direct ownership of enterprises and price and wage controls. On the other hand, it has to increase its role in areas where it has been rather inactive. They are income distribution policy through taxation, an increase of social welfare programmes, the regulation of pollution and more active environmental programmes. This kind of shift requires a major restructuring of government organisation and the retraining of government officials. But the government has been very slow to act.

III: THE GOVERNMENT REGULATION OF *CHAEBOL*

An alternative to active government intervention in the Korean economy is to give more freedom to big business groups, the *chaebol*. But these business groups are far from popular among the general populace. In fact, many social problems are associated with them. A recent survey about the perception of big business groups reveals that they have a serious image problem among their own people. People were asked which words came to their minds when asked about *chaebol*. Some of the negative images included speculation on real estate, the excessive concentration of economic power, too much diversification of business lines, inadequate concern about the environment, poor management–labour relations, and the concentration of ownership and managerial control in the hands of a few families. The negative image and social criticisms of big business are certainly not a healthy sign of the Korean capitalist system. In this section, two aspects of *chaebol* criticisms will be discussed in more detail.

The central issue of the *chaebol* question is the dual control of business firms through ownership and managerial governance. Based on the efficiency criterion alone, one cannot make a clear case of which system is better. On the one extreme, we have the situation of the Korean *chaebol* where there is no separation of ownership and management.[4] The system guarantees the stability of management and also enables companies to undertake the big or risky projects which are necessary for the national economy. When big business groups dominate the economy, however, they tend to pre-empt resources and build formidable entry barriers to aspiring firms. This will tend to reduce competition in the overall economy, although competition could still be fierce among a small number of companies in particular product markets. There is also a possibility of unfair competition because the member companies of a group could cross-subsidise each other or provide unfair privileges to sister companies in terms of price and payment terms.

At the other extreme lies the American system where there is an almost complete separation of ownership and control. Business managers tend to be very short-term oriented because the evaluation and remuneration of the managers is structured in such a way as to favour short-term profits. In addition, there is an emphasis on merger, acquisition and corporate takeovers which do not directly help to strengthen the fundamental competitive capabilities of firms. In other words, business units are often viewed as parts of a portfolio and financial considerations are given a top priority relative to technology or marketing. This tendency is often considered one of the reasons why American companies are losing ground in the global competition. There are nevertheless efficient aspects to the American system in which mismanaged companies are eliminated from the market in a relatively short period of time and capital investment is constantly shifted to industries which promise the highest profits.

In between these two systems lies the Japanese structure which is often called 'corporate capitalism'. There is separation of ownership and management; particular individuals or families have such a small percentage of the stocks of major corporations that they do not have a controlling influence over the management of the companies. Instead, companies in loose business groups (called *keiretsu*) hold each other's stocks, thus maintaining stability in the managerial control of the companies. Since these institutional stockholders are not that interested in short-term profits, companies tend to be more long-term oriented and emphasise market share. And these companies can undertake investments which require a rather long gestation period. The Japanese corporate system seems to be both efficient and socially acceptable.

A criticism of the ownership structure of Korean *chaebol* is based on the equity argument rather than the efficiency argument. It is unacceptable for many Korean people that such huge assets and resources are in the hands of several powerful families. As long as this perception persists among the Korean people, big business will continue to be criticised for many social problems and be used as a scapegoat in politically unstable periods, such as in the early 1990s. Then how could this problem be solved? Unless there is a revolutionary situation such as the US occupation of Japan at the end of the Second World War, during which the Americans dissolved the Japanese *zaibatsu*, change in the ownership structure of Korean business groups could be only very gradual.[5] In the long run, there will be several factors which will result in the gradual separation of ownership and management. First, as inheritance and gift taxes are administered more strictly, inter-generational wealth transfer will be more difficult and costly. Second, the future growth and expansion of business firms will require the selling of stocks to outside independent stockholders and this will dilute the stock ownership of large shareholders. Third, owner managers are delegating authority to professional managers in order to recruit the best people and keep them highly motivated. It is already happening in many big business groups that owner managers are trying to limit the participation of their own family members in the day-to-day operations of companies. Fourth, it is likely that the government will continue to implement progressive measures that could facilitate the separation of ownership and management. The limitation of cross-holding among sister companies, currently in effect, is one such example. Another example is the recent government policy of discriminating among business groups, in the bank credit regulations, depending on the degrees of ownership concentration by owner families. The more dispersed the ownership of a corporation is, the less restrictive credit regulation will apply. It may still take a generation for all these factors to have a significant impact on the ownership pattern of Korean business groups. In the meantime, it is likely that criticisms and controversies concerning big business groups in Korea will continue.

Another issue that is often discussed in relation to big business groups is the diversification of business lines. *Chaebols* are often criticised for their over-extended lines of business. It is often claimed that an unrelated diversification strategy brings about many second-class companies rather than a few world-class companies. In an era of global competition, also-rans cannot survive very long and Korean big business groups cannot serve their country if they fail to stand up to the global competition. This line of argument seems to be a logical one, although it is not easy to prove the hypothesis with empirical data. Global competition will gradually force Korean companies to be more selective in their product-market decisions, although there is a strong inertia in these groups to perpetuate excessively diversified business portfolios. A recent controversy about the diversification issue is whether the government should intervene.[6] Suffice to say that government intervention in corporate diversification strategy could result in the diminution of competition in the affected industries. Following the logic of the previous section, the government should not be involved directly in areas which belong to corporate decisions. Instead, the government should set broad guidelines and rules by which business firms should operate. If the government maintains an open-door policy to foreign companies and also eliminates various artificial entry barriers, business groups will be forced to be more strategic in the selection of business areas.

The general conclusion is that the *chaebol* structure is very much imbedded in the Korean economy and that it is not likely to change dramatically in the near future. The question still remains: as an alternative to potentially inefficient government intervention in the market, are the *chaebols* reliable and efficient enough to entrust the economic future of the nation? Popular feeling seems to be that they are not very trustworthy. Given the fact that the government has played such an important role in Korean economic growth, private business firms are not likely to have the full confidence of the people.

IV: NEW BUSINESS–GOVERNMENT RELATIONS

The argument so far can be summarised by three points. First, the Korean economy has been characterised by heavy government intervention during the last three decades. Government–business relations in Korea should be clearly distinguished from other Asian NIEs, despite a myth presented by some Western economists who try to picture Korea and Taiwan as cases of a free market economy. Heavy government intervention has often resulted in the misallocation of resources and market distortions toward the second half of the last three decades. Second, close government–business relations are partially supported by the *kwan-kei* culture in Korea. There are continuous and very close relations between business managers and government officials based on primary group relations. Third, Korean big business groups are certainly not popular among the general public. In the transitional period of democratisation after 1987, the government in the Sixth Republic has attempted to regulate the *chaebol*. This attempt has been dubbed a 'new industrial policy' by the Korean press in the 1992 election year. The new industrial policy has never been clearly defined by the government, but it has been interpreted as meaning the government's attempt to regulate *chaebol* particularly in the areas of ownership structure and diversification strategy. As was implied above, the government regulation of *chaebol* will result in another round of market distortions and inefficiencies. There is no clear-cut case where a particular ownership structure of diversification strategy is superior to others. The best structure and strategy are the ones that enhance global competitiveness. There is no guarantee that government direct intervention in the corporate structure will result in the improvement of corporate performance. It is the market which determines the best form of ownership structure and diversification strategy.

The best government policy is to reduce government intervention. The first priority should be to liberalise regulation in the financial market. The financial sector is probably the most heavily regulated industry in the Korean economy and at the same time the most backward industry. All operations from entry to interest rate determinations are heavily regulated by the Ministry of Finance. The Ministry may be the most conservative among economic ministries and also the most inward-looking. The question is how one goes about liberalising a sector in which the *status quo* is maintained by implicit collusion between the Ministry and managers of financial institutions. The collusion is partially maintained by the *kwan-kei* culture mentioned above and also by the fact that existing financial institutions are benefiting greatly by entry regulation. This government–business complex is very difficult to break up without strong pressure from outside. This is why Korea needs outside leverage and pressures for the opening up of the market to foreign competition. One may argue that nothing is wrong with current government intervention in Korea. After all, the Korean economy has shown one of the best macroeconomic performances in the world in the last three decades. On the other hand, one can also argue that, without the heavy government intervention, the Korean economy may have performed even better. In fact, compared to Taiwan, Korea has performed poorly in major macroeconomic indicators such as inflation and balance of payments. The difference in performance can be partially attributable to the heavier government intervention in Korea compared to Taiwan. There are at least five reasons why Taiwan has performed better than Korea. They are (i) better initial conditions (in the early 1950s) and more successful agricultural land reforms; (ii) flexibility and the fast response of small businesses to changing market conditions overseas; (iii) the presence of overseas Chinese assisting investment and overseas connections; (iv) the earlier opening up of domestic markets and market liberalisation; and (v) less intervention by the government in the economy. It can be seen that the last two reasons, market opening and market liberalisation, are controllable by the government.[7]

It is argued here that the excessive intervention in market mechanisms and the protection of domestic industries by the government are two major hindrances to the further upgrading of the Korean economy. At the early stage of industrialisation, when economic growth was achieved through the extensive use of resources (meaning simply the mobilising of idle resources such as unskilled labour and the setting up of production facilities using imported technology), government intervention may have exerted a positive impact on economic growth. But at the later stage when growth should come from a higher level of technology, the upgrading of human skills and, most of all, the sophisticated management of various business functions, the government can easily become a hindrance on the road to the efficiency.

There was one incident in 1992 which could fundamentally change business–government relations in Korea. The founder and chairman of the biggest *chaebol* in Korea, Hyundai's Chung Ju Yung, organised a political party and obtained more than 15 per cent of the popular vote in the general election of 1992. This has never happened before in the history of Korea. Traditionally, business was placed under government bureaucrats who were in turn subject to the control of the political elite. The traditionally vertical relationship among three elites (power elite, bureaucrats and business) has been turned upside down, as a *chaebol* tycoon joined the ranks of the political elite.

Although the presidential bid by Chung failed by a wide margin (he was a distant third in the presidential election in December 1992), the episode had some implications for the long-term relationship between business and government. First, it showed that the business sector has achieved a somewhat higher status *vis-à-vis* the government. Since the transfer of power has been regularly and peacefully made in the political arena since 1988, the tenure of political positions is limited. This is compared to the position of owner managers whose tenures are unlimited. This may be one reason why the relative position of business managers has been upgraded compared to politicians or bureaucrats. Second, as the tenure of politicians is limited, career bureaucrats started to dissociate themselves from politically appointed ministers and other high governmental officers. In other words, the political elite, career civil servants and business owners will maintain more independent positions. This means that bureaucrats will attempt to control businesses as much as possible, because it is their source of power. This could develop into a chain of control as in Japan. That is, business is controlled by bureaucrats, bureaucrats are controlled by the political parties and lastly politicians are strongly influenced by business because of their need for political funds. Third, a split developed among business groups during the presidential election, because different business groups lined up with different political parties. Business and government relationships in Korea have often been called 'Korea, Inc.'. It was often mentioned that 'Korea, Inc.' is more tightly knit and more vertical than 'Japan, Inc.'. This was true as long as the political elite, especially military generals turned presidents, was in firm control of the economy. In fact, the whole economy was organised like a company, and different business groups worked in harmony under the guidance of the president. Now that the vertical relationship does not work as it used to, horizontal relationships among business groups themselves will reveal more competition and, at times, conflicts.

After the Kim Young Sam Administration took office in February 1993, there were a few new developments which could affect business–government relations in the future. First of all, President Kim declared that he will not receive any financial contribution from business during his tenure as president. It is widely known that previous presidents regularly received large sums of money from big business groups and used them for political purposes. If this promise is maintained, it will fundamentally affect government–business relations. A new election law was also passed by the National Assembly in early 1994. The law contains strict rules which limit the amount of political contributions candidates can receive from business. Although the president tried to dissociate himself from the business sector financially, he has maintained a favourable stance towards the big business groups. Although there were some discussions about measures to regulate *chaebol* during the early period of his presidency, these discussions were not followed by concrete steps either to separate the ownership and control of big business or to force them to specialise in limited areas of production. On the contrary, as the goal of regaining international competitiveness in the world market becomes the primary goal of the government, several large corporations such as Samsung Electronics and Kia Motors are treated as national champions who represent Korea in the world market. In addition, the government has attempted to deregulate the whole economy after it took office. Although it will take some time before the bureaucrats retreat from the areas in which they have been involved for such a long time, there is at least a wide consensus that over-regulation of the business sector has hampered the international competitiveness of Korean companies. If all these changes under the Kim administration take effect, the tightly controlled, vertical business–government relations in Korea that have been developed between the 1960s and the 1980s could finally be replaced by a more independent and horizontal relationship between the two.

V: CONCLUDING REMARKS

Looking into the 1990s and beyond, there are at least three factors that will further change traditional business–government relations in Korea. First, the opening up of the domestic market will have an affect. Multinational corporations account for a small share of the Korean economy currently, but their share will slowly grow in the future as the restrictions on inward direct investment are lifted by the government. Foreign companies already operating in the country usually demand internationally accepted rules and regulations and they also seek the rule-based regulation of business through legislation or decrees instead of administrative guidance. This is happening already in the banking sector as well as in the advertising industry. The presence of a foreign business community will affect the overall regulation of the economy by government, since the latter has to treat the domestic and foreign business sector on the same basis.

The second factor which will affect business–government relations in Korea is the localisation of government. There will be a popular election of provincial governors for the first time in 35 years in 1995. Candidates for local government heads are expected to promise more economic prosperity for their regions, which will be translated into more favourable environments for business. In other words, provinces and cities are expected to compete with each other to attract more business to their regions. In addition, the decentralisation of economic decision making to local governments will erode the power that is currently held by economic ministries of the central government. This will in turn loosen the current tight relationship between economic ministries and business groups.

Thirdly, a new social and political environment will also influence the business–government relationship in the future. It is noteworthy that the first civilian president was elected in 1992 after 31 years of rule by presidents with a military background. As democracy takes a firmer root in the country, it is expected that different environments will emerge for business. The government is expected to be only one of many stakeholders in business. Labour unions have now become a legitimate and important part of society. Voluntary citizens' organisations with such causes as consumer protection and environmental protection have become more vocal. Banks and financial institutions have become more independent. The press and other mass media have become a force that the business community has to deal with every day. In other words, business now has to cope with multiple stakeholders, whereas in the old authoritarian days the government was really the only important force outside business.[8]

All these three factors and others such as the globalisation of Korean business itself are expected to change the traditional 'Korea, Inc.' model of business–government relations. But, at the same time, cultures and traditions linger on, and the tightly knit social fabric and the Confucian tradition of giving high social status to civil servants are expected to maintain the traditionally important role of the government in society. The next ten years will show us more clearly in which direction the business–government relationship will evolve in Korea.

NOTES

1. K-H. Jung, 'Business–Government Relations in the Growth of Korean Business Groups', *Korean Social Science Journal*, Vol.14 (1988), pp.67–82.
2. C. Wolf, *Market and Government: Choosing Between Imperfect Markets* (Camb., Mass., 1990).
3. F. Deyo (ed.), *The Political Economy of the New Asian Industrialism* (Ithaca, 1987); G. White (ed.) *Developmental States in East Asia* (London, 1988). See also C. Johnson, *MITI and the Japanese Miracle* (Stanford, 1972).
4. See O.E. Williamson, *Markets and Hierarchies: Analysis and Antitrust Implications* (New York, 1975).
5. G.G. Hamilton and M. Orru, 'Organisational Structure of East Asian Companies', in K.H. Chung and H.C. Lee (eds.), *Korean Managerial Dynamics* (New York, 1989), pp.39–50.
6. K-H. Jung, *Diversification Strategies and the International Competitiveness of Korean Business* (in Korean) (Seoul, 1991).
7. B. Levy, 'Korean and Taiwanese Firms as International Competitors: the Challenges Ahead', *Columbia Journal of World Business* (1988), pp.43–51.
8. K-H. Jung, 'Economic Reforms in Korea: In Search of a New Role for the Government, Business and the Market', in D. Kim *et al.* (eds.), *The Role of Market and State: Economic and Social Reforms in East Asia and East-Central Europe* (Seoul, 1991), pp.91–108.

The Evolving Role of Government in China's Transitional Economy

JOHN WONG and KANG CHEN

I: GOVERNMENT IN ECONOMIC TRANSITION

China started its economic reform and open-door policy in 1979. By October 1992, when the 14th Congress of the Chinese Communist Party (CCP) formally endorsed the concept of 'socialist market economy' the Chinese economy in terms of its structure and institutional condition had changed almost beyond recognition. The traditional role and function of government geared to the original socialist system had also undergone tremendous change. When a socialist economy takes to market reform in earnest, it is characterised as a 'transitional economy'. According to Paul Streeten,[1] the government of such a transitional economy (including any of the former socialist countries in eastern Europe) has to address three important questions concerning the nature and extent of government intervention in economic life: (1) how to manage the transition from excessive to reduced government intervention; (2) how to shift from interventions in the wrong areas to those in previously neglected important ones; and (3) how to change from one form of economic management (reliance on planning or quantitative controls) to another (reliance on prices as instruments of policy). In the case of an Asian transitional economy such as China or Vietnam, both classified as manifestly backward, we may add the fourth question pertaining to the 'developmental role of the government'. Whereas the governments of the European socialist economies need only tackle the task of transforming their socialistic structures towards the more efficient market-based systems, the governments of Asian transitional economies are faced with the additional burden of de-socialising and industralising at the same time. The role and function of the Chinese government is therefore much more complicated. Apart from playing out the 'reformist role' as outlined by Streeten, it is also expected to fulfil its 'developmental functions'.

China has made significant progress in addressing these issues during its reform process over the past 15 years. The previously all-encompassing role of government has indeed been greatly reduced, mandatory plans abolished, prices decontrolled, and administrative controls decentralised. Along with the reform of the incentive structures and resource allocation pattern, the Chinese government's overall economic role has become

John Wong, Institute of East Asian Political Economy, Singapore; Kang Chen, Nanyang Technological University.

more 'market-friendly'.[2] These changes unleashed the latent entre-preneurial energies of the Chinese people and led to increases in productivity and efficiency. Consequently, the Chinese economy has experienced spectacular growth at near double-digit rates during 1979–93 (see Table 1).

However, China, on account of its being a 'half-reformed economy', has addressed these issues only partially, with many problems still outstanding. For instance, macroeconomic management still relies very much on administrative controls; many social services such as housing, health, pension, and unemployment benefits are still provided by enterprises; and the state-owned enterprises (SOEs) remain subject to rigid government interference in day-to-day operations. Such an outcome is not surprising if one bears in mind the open-ended nature of China's economic reform, which precludes the need to map out a detailed reform progress plan and to lay down the necessary role and functions of the government. But more complications have arisen with the recent adoption of the concept of 'socialist market economy'. Does the principle of 'socialist market economy' embrace the progressive reduction of the government's dominant role in the economy while maintaining predominant public ownership at the same time? The exact role of the government in the 'socialist market economy' has remained undefined. Lieberthal and Oksenberg[3] have pointed out that the bureaucratic structure in China is fragmented and its policy process protracted, disjointed, and incremental. Its structure of authority requires that any major decision or policy initiative has to gain the active cooperation of sectoral and regional adminstrators, and that a consensus must be sought both horizontally and vertically in the system. This explains why the Chinese local governments are playing an increasingly important role. It is therefore important to extend the scope of this study to cover the evolving role of government at the sub-national levels.

II: THE PRE-REFORM SOCIALISTIC ROLE

Compared with the highly centralised former Soviet Union, the scope of China's mandatory planning in the pre-reform period of 1949–78 covered much fewer categories of commodities, while China's local governments took much more active role in the formulation and interpretation of plans. Nevertheless, the Chinese economic system was still basically a Soviet-type system in terms of its functional organisations. In such a system, the control and priorities of the central political leadership are maintained through a vast and complex structure of overlapping administrative hierarchies, which are set up to gather information, disseminate instructions, coordinate interactions, and monitor and enforce compliance and performance.[4] Within such a system, the Communist Party comprises the highest authority and its central organs exercise real

TABLE 1

ECONOMIC AND SOCIAL STATISTICS OF CHINA AND SELECTED
ASIA-PACIFIC COUNTRIES

	Area 1000s per sq.km.	Population m 1991	Total GNP $USm 1991	Nominal GNP per capita $US 1991
China	9561	1150	369,651	370
Japan	378	124	3,362,282	26,930
NIE				
S.Korea	99	43	282,970	6,330
Taiwan	36	21	181,230	8,815
Hong Kong	1	6	67,555	13,430
Singapore	1	3	39,983	14,210
ASEAN (*)				
Brunei	6	0.3	na	21,000
Indonesia	1,905	181	116,476	610
Malaysia	330	18	46,980	2,520
Philippines	300	63	44,908	730
Thailand	513	57	na	1,570

| | Real GDP Growth (%) | | | | | |
	1960-70	1970-80	1980-90	1991	1992	1993
China	5.2	5.8	9.5	7.0	12.8	13.0
Japan	10.9	5.0	4.1	3.4	0.9	-0.6
NIE						
S.Korea	8.6	9.5	9.7	8.3	4.8	5.4
Taiwan	9.2	9.7	7.1	7.2	6.6	6.0
Hong Kong	10.0	9.3	7.1	4.0	5.0	5.3
Singapore	8.8	8.5	6.4	6.9	5.8	8.8
ASEAN (*)						
Brunei	na	na	na	3.5	3.0	na
Indonesia	3.9	7.6	5.5	5.3	5.8	7.1
Malaysia	6.5	7.8	5.2	8.3	8.0	8.7
Philippines	5.1	6.3	0.9	1.0	0.0	0.9
Thailand	8.4	7.2	7.6	7.9	7.4	7.5

	Annual Export Growth (%) 1965-80 1980-91		Manufacturing Exports as % of Total Resources 1991	Foreign Exchange US$bn 1992
China	5.5	11.5	83	47
Japan	11.4	4.0	98	73
NIE				
S.Korea	27.2	12.2	93	17
Taiwan	28.5	16.0	93	82
Hong Kong	9.1	4.4	95	35
Singapore	4.7	8.9	74	40
ASEAN (*)				
Brunei	na	na	na	na
Indonesia	9.6	4.5	41	10
Malaysia	4.6	10.9	61	17
Philippines	4.6	3.3	71	4
Thailand	8.6	14.4	66	20

* Singapore is also a member of ASEAN

Source: *World Development Report* (1960–93); *The Statistical Yearbook of the Republic of China* (Taipei, 1993); ADB, Asian Development Outlook and *The Straits Times* (Singapore, 13 April 1994).

political power. The Party's structure and its functionaries are tightly interwoven with those of the governmental system. The central government and its array of central planning and control agencies are responsible for translating the objectives and policies of the political authorities into plans, implementation assignments and instructions. This top-down system of control is supported by the regionally based system of control from duplicated organs at every level of the administrative hierarchy. Thus, resource allocation is done by physical planning and administrative rationing.

Musgrave[5] distinguished the three economic activities of government: economic stabilisation, allocation, and redistribution. Broadly speaking, the economic role of China's socialist government had followed much the same lines. But the CCP had placed greater emphasis on price stability, full employment, and income equality. To achieve these three goals the Chinese planners sought to mobilise resources and allocate them by relying on three major instruments: price control, enterprise control and planning control.

Price Control

China's administrative price system in the pre-reform period was primarily used for measurement, accounting control and income redistribution purposes. Prices, wages and salaries were administratively set and controlled by the government. In order to maintain price stablity, prices remained fixed for extremely long periods, leading to a price structure which could not reflect changing demand, opportunity costs, and the relative scarcity relationship among commodities. Furthermore, the government deliberately turned the terms of trade against agricultural products and raw materials, including energy, by keeping their prices relatively low and the prices of manufactured goods relatively high. This pricing policy had made it possible to implement the 'low income, low consumption, high employment' policy, which fulfilled the official objective of egalitarianism with the standard of living of the majority of the population pegged at the subsistence level. It had also helped to keep production costs low so the state could skim off the surplus to finance capital construction in industrial sectors. Here, price control actually functioned as an *implicit* taxation system which used SOEs (industrial firms, agricultural procurement agencies, foreign trade companies, and so on) as tax-collecting vehicles.[6] All enterprises' 'profits' – really residual cash surpluses – simply reverted to the state.

Enterprise Control

Enterprises, be they state-owned or collectively owned, were all closely controlled by government agencies. The SOEs received resources and carried out the actual production according to the central plan. Even their fixed investments were subjected to government control through investment plans. Under such a system, it is clearly in the collective interest of the enterprise managers and their subordinates to under-report or underestimate the productive potential of their enterprises and to overestimate their resources requirement so that their production targets could be set at such a low level as to be easily fulfilled, leaving the extra resources for their personal uses. Hence, there exists a great tendency at all levels to monopolise the information on the extra output obtainable from assigned resources.[7] Therefore, enterprise surpluses remain uncertain even under centralised price and output controls. As mentioned previously, enterprises were used as tax-collecting vehicles by the state. Enforcing revenue collection in the case of uncertainty would require that 'unexpected' surpluses remain 'blocked' as they were generated *ex post*.[8] Hence, enterprise deposits in the state bank could not even be spent on domestic goods and services without permission, nor were enterprises allowed to hold 'cash' (coin and currrency) that could be spent without being traced. This 'blocked' enterprise money was carefully monitored by the state bank to prevent it from converting into wages for household consumption. Hence enterprise control is also linked to wage controls.

Planning Control

Central planning involves coordinating hundreds of thousands of operational units with numerous production and distribution processes and numerous products. It also covers investment, employment, income distribution, and consumption. At the macro level, this involves balancing the state budget, bank loans, demand for foreign exchange, regional and sectoral growth, and so on. The actual process of planning requires iterative communication and bargaining among the central agencies and along the economic chain of command within each sector of the economy. Thus politics is allowed to creep into the planning process, which along with distorted information can result in the formulation of inconsistent or even unworkable plans at the operational level. Therefore, frequent administrative orders have to be issued to facilitate the implementation of the plans.

In addition to these means of controls, everybody has to belong to a unit (or *danwei* in Chinese), which provides a lifetime job, housing, health care, pension, and other welfare benefits. Therefore, the unit has ultimate control on the overall well-being of its members. Every unit is assigned a rank in the hierarchical structure and enjoys certain power and privileges according to its relative position in the structure. It was through such direct control of the units that the Chinese government had asserted its all-embracing role in the political and economic life of the pre-reform China.

It may be stressed that Mao Zedong himself soon became disenchanted with the highly centralised Soviet-type planning system so he launched the Great Leap Forward movement in 1958. His decentralisation drive sought to expand the autonomy of local governments and reduce the complexity and scope of central plans and directives, thereby rationalising the economic environment in which subordinates had to operate. However, as enterprises and local governments were given greater autonomy in a world of arbitrary administrative prices, they increasingly engaged in what Ericson calls 'dysfunctional behaviour',[9] by making wrong investments and the wrong assortment of output. The centre was then compelled to backtrack on the decentralisation reform, and started to re-centralise investment, to increase the detail and constraints of central plans, and to tighten control over supply allocations. Accordingly, from the late 1950s to the mid-1970s, China witnessed repeated cycles of decentralisation and recentralisation. Repeated administrative decentralisation in the pre-1978 period had resulted in the expansion of extrabudgetary revenue of local governments and the development of rural industrial enterprises, and both of which, in retrospect, have served as important facilitators in China's reform process.[10]

III: NEW ROLES IN THE REFORM ERA

The economic role of government everywhere is continuously changing in response to changing social preferences and political needs.[11] This is especially the case for China's economic reform process which was initiated top-down by the CCP. The political forces within the CCP at the inception of reform can be divided into three major groups according to their political and economic attitudes: the democratic reformers, the authoritarian reformers, and the conservatives.[12] The democratic reformers supported market-oriented reforms; but they also promoted various degrees of democratisation.[13] The authoritarian reformers were the original proponents of market-oriented reforms but they did not want to have any basic change in the existing political system. They could envisage a 'marriage' between political dictatorship and economic freedom.[14] The conservatives opposed both market-oriented economic reform and political changes, although they were willing to improve central planning and control by reducing the detail and scope of plans and directives.[15]

The interplay among these three groups of political forces can explain most of the changes in the economic role of government in the reform era. Learning from the lessons and experiences of the past decentralisation–recentralisation cycles, the authoritarian reformers came to recognise that partial reforms within the old planning framework would no longer suffice, and that market-oriented reform would be the only way out for China. In order to push for market-oriented reform, the authoritarian reformers would need to form a 'united front' with the democractic reformers to engage in the so-called 'thought liberalising movement'. But, on the other hand, the authoritarian reformers would endorse only the liberation of 'economic thoughts', but not the 'undesirable demands' for political reforms and democracy. Therefore, the authoritarian reformers were prepared to team up with the conservatives to contain the democratic reformers. Deng Xiaoping summarised it as 'opposing dogmatism in the economic sphere from the left, and combatting bourgeois liberalism in the political and ideological sphere from the right.'[16] In maintaining the balance the authoritarian reformers (who prevailed most of the time) had to form coalitions with either the democratic reformers or the conservatives from time to time, and hence the different outcomes for different time periods.

1979–83

The 1979–83 period was basically dominated by the coalition between the authoritarian reformers and the conservatives. At the beginning of the period, the authoritarian reformers tried to set marketisation as the main direction of reform,[17] but they had met strong resistance from the conservatives. In the end, market-oriented reform was not sanctioned by the CCP in its 12th Congress held in 1982. It appeared that the authoritarian reformers had not gained enough political strength at that time. By compromising with the conservatives, they were able to gain some ground in controlling key positions in the Party and the state. In addition, consensus was reached within the Party to pursue partial reform along the lines of decentralisation. Thus, the scope of planning was reduced and the prices of some consumer goods were decontrolled. And, most importantly, a budgetary arrangement was introduced under which local governments were given specific tax bases as their own and were made responsible for meeting revenue targets and for the outcomes of their respective budgets.[18] The incentives induced by this budgetary arrangement has since played an important role in China's reform process.

An important and yet unexpected outcome of decentralisation in China has been rural 'decollectivisation'. Contrary to the popular belief, rural reforms were never 'planned' by the government. When communes and production brigades were given more autonomy in making production decisions in 1979, land tenure and the household contract system were immediately initiated by farmers in poor and remote areas and spread quickly to other areas. Initially opposing these changes, the government gradually recognised that these innovations had wide support and could help solve the acute problem of grain supply shortage. And it was not until 1985 that the government sanctioned the key administrative measures that comprised China's successful rural reforms.[19] The implication of rural decollectivisation is tremendous: it greatly reduced government control in the economic life of rural society.

1984–88

For most of the 1984–88 period, the authoritarian reformers were able to work with the democratic reformers and market-oriented reform was formally endorsed by the Party. This was reflected in the 'Decision on Reform of the Economic Structures', adopted by the Third Plenary Session of the 12th Party Congress in 1984, stating that the Chinese economy would move toward a 'planned commodity economy'.[20] It was further explained in the 13th Party Congress held in 1987 that the state should play an indirect role in economic management: 'the state regulates the market while the market guides the enterprises'. The role of the state was to change from one of planning and directing economic resources to one that would manage the policies of resource allocation.

Accordingly, China's reform quickly moved into new arena, including the introduction of the two-tier pricing system. Enterprises, after fulfilling official contracts with fixed prices, could now trade above-quota amounts of products in the open market at flexible prices. The two-tier pricing system has been particularly effective in broadening capital goods markets, which did not exist in the previous period. It has also enabled the rural industrial enterprises to gain access to the much needed capital goods, so facilitating the rapid growth of rural TVEs. However, the two-tier pricing system soon gave rise to a lot of problems including widespread rent-seeking activities and downright corruption. In particular, government officials were able to abuse their power for profiteering by acquiring goods in short supply at the state fixed prices from enterprises and reselling them at exorbitant market prices.[21]

In retrospect, Chinese economists were divided over the two-tier system. One influential group called for a comprehensive reform package comprising price, tax, financial, fiscal, domestic and foreign trade reforms so as to provide a rational macroeconomic environment for enterprises to operate.[22] The other group emphasised rationalising the micro-foundation of the economy and thus making enterprises responsive to market signals, and they argued for enterprise ownership reforms such as introducing the share-holding system and corporatising the state enterprises.[23]

Corruption and profiteering by government officials also heightened the debate on political reform. The authoritarian reformers now saw the greater need for administrative reforms in the sense of establishing a professional civil service system, and separating the functions of the Party organs from the governmental organs. The democratic reformers advocated a more fundamental reform of the political system, with some of them even going so far as to demand a Western form of democracy based on a multiparty system, complete with freedom of the press. Their views were particularly popular among intellectuals and students and gave rise to the pro-democracy movement by students at the end of 1986. Alarmed by the potential spread of instability, the conservatives and the authoritarian reformers joined forces to oppose such 'bourgeois liberalisation', resulting in the purge of a number of the leading democratic reformers and forcing the liberal Party General Secretary, Hu Yaobang, to step down. The democratic reformers have since lost their influence at the top level.

1989-92

With the purge of the democratic reformers, reform was indeed put on hold. The lack of reform progress aggravated the frictions between plan and market, and such problems as inflation and corruption eventually led to widespread social discontent and the pro-democracy movement in the spring of 1989. After the Tianamen tragedy, the political pendulum swung to the conservatives' side, with some authoritarian reformers themselves becoming the targets of the purge. Party General-Secretary Zhao Ziyang was accused of 'supporting bourgeois liberalism', and 'bringing reform into the orbit of capitalism'. Zhao was stripped of all posts in the Party and the government. Zhao's close supporters were criticised, demoted, or purged. The Chinese newspapers in the aftermath of the Tianamen event published articles criticising the market-oriented reforms. Attempts were also made by the central government to expand the scope of the mandatory plan and to promote the SOEs, and to restrict the growth of private enterprises including rural TVEs. These policies were later adopted by the 5th Plenary Session of the 13th Central Committee of the CCP held in December 1989. However, such re-centralisation efforts were not successfully carried out for fear of causing massive unemployment problems and more fiscal deficits.[24] Actually, the decentalisation–recentralisation cycle has already been broken by the 'self-reinforcing nature of reform'.[25] The conservatives finally came to realise that it was not possible to preserve their interests by reversing reforms and re-introducing planning. In the meantime, a bottom-up reform pattern had emerged as many local governments continued to carry out 'unsanctioned' reforms in their localities in order to protect their own economic interests, and as the central leadership was unable to give new directions. The reform deadlock at the centre was eventually brought to an end in early 1992 when Deng Xiaoping, in his historic tour of South China, called for an all-out effort to speed up the reform and hence delivered his 'final blow' at the planned economy. Deng's new initiative, in retrospect, reignited the reform momentum, culminating in the adoption by the 14th Party Congress of the 'socialist market economy' as the objective of China's economic reform.

Overview

In summary, it is difficullt to delineate exactly the changing role of the government in the reform process. The changes have been partial, incremental, experimental, and at times even back-tracking. But the overall direction of changes has been unmistakable: the economic role of government has been changed significantly in the following five areas:

- Price control has been greatly reduced. By the end of 1993 the prices of 90 per cent of consumer goods and over 80 per cent of intermediate goods were no longer fixed by the state but set by market forces.[26]
- Enterprise autonomy has been expanded. State firms can now independently make decisions to change output quantity and variety, production technology, bonuses to workers, and to some degree output prices.
- Economic planning has largely lost its relevance in guiding the macroeconomy. Production plans and materials allocation plans now affect less than 20 per cent of production and material distribution, and planned macroeconomic targets are not seriously implemented (see Table 2).
- The government's role as a producer has been dramatically curtailed. The share of the SOEs in total industrial output fell from 78 per cent in 1978 to 48 per cent in 1992. The non-state sector, on the other hand, has experienced a rapid expansion.
- The government's role as a financier of investment has also been greatly decreased as the role of budgetary financing has declined. In 1978, about 40 per cent of the SOE's investment came from the state budget. By 1989, this share fell to only 13 per cent.

While the economic role of central government has been greatly reduced, much of the discretion has shifted to local governments. It is therefore important to take into account the evolving roles of Chinese local government in the process of economic reform.

IV: DECENTRALISATION AND LOCAL GOVERNMENTS

Two basic types of decentralisation can be distinguished: administrative decentralisation with powers devolving from the centre to lower levels of administration (local governments or local branches of central agencies), and economic decentralisation with powers of planning, coordination and management of the administrative units devolving to enterprises.[27] Both types of decentralisation formed an integral part of economic reform. Administrative decentralisation was a means of using locally available information more effectively, of allowing local preferences to have greater influence over local spending decisions, and of providing material incentives to local governments and enterprises to pursue growth objectives. But administrative decentralisation alone does not necessarily imply an immediate transition to a market economy. In many former

TABLE 2

PLANNED AND ACTUAL ECONOMIC INDICATORS IN 1993

	Planned	Actual
GNP	8%	13%
Industry (value added)	14%	21%
Fixed investment	10%	51%
Trade volume (exports plus imports)	12%	18%
Retail price index	6%	13%
Currency in circulation (bn yuan)	100	153
New bank loans (bn yuan)	380	483

Source: Dong Furen, 'Can China Stabilise its Economy in 1994', Lianhe Zaobao, 16 March 1994.

socialist economies, this merely resulted in 'decentralising' industry without concomitant managerial autonomy or incentives like private property rights. Therefore, economic decentralisation is of intrinsic importance in the market transition. The goal here is to create institutions conducive to market activities so that profit-maximising economic agents can better respond to market signals and make decisions independently. However, the past experience in China has shown that administrative decentralisation could run into conflict with economic decentralisation. Progress toward the objective of increasing enterprise autonomy would naturally entail a diminution in the authority of local governments. Therefore, local governments had to resort to their 'innovative ways' of retaining power. They could 'recapture' control over enterprises through a variety of informal mechanisms, as well as through control over geographically immobile factors and resources.[28] This resulted in the two major dilemmas which stemmed from decentralisation.[29]

The Fiscal Decentralisation Dilemma

Under the 'Centre–Local Revenue Sharing System' introduced in 1980, local governments were given specific shares of financial revenues; and were made responsible for meeting revenue targets of the central government. Since the centre has different interests and objectives from those of local governments, there has been intense bargaining between the centre and local governments over revenue sharing. Local governments would negotiate with the centre for a more favourable revenue-sharing ratio, a bigger subsidy from the centre, or a reduction in expenditure responsibilities. Because they were in charge of tax collection and administration, local governments could also pursue tax evasion or avoidance tactics to keep resources within their locality, rather than sharing them with the centre. Funds 'stored' in this way in the enterprises could then be transferred to local governments by *ad hoc* levies.[30] By linking local revenues directly to enterprise income, fiscal decentralisation thus had the effect of pushing the SOEs into the arms of local governments. Participation of local officials in enterprise operations perpetuates the problem of bureaucratic management and the tendency to shield enterprises from market discipline. In the end, it cancels out some of the original intentions of economic decentralisation: that of increasing enterprise autonomy and insulating their operations from government interference.

Financial Decentralisation Dilemma

Currently, a larger share of investment in China is being financed through bank loans rather than through government budgets. This, however, should not be viewed as evidence of true financial autonomy. The increasing share of investment financed by bank loans merely reflects the increasing influence of local governments on investment decisions. At the beginning of reform, the government budget was the principal instrument for mobilising surplus for direct investment. Over the years, these responsibilities have come to rest more heavily on the household and enterprise sectors, with a major intermediation role to be played by the financial sector. The reform has allowed enterprises to retain profits and surpluses and keep them in their bank accounts. In theory, banks are then in a position to intermediate these funds, and to channel them to profitable investments.

Under the close supervision of local governments, however, local banks actually have limited scope for independent decisions, partly because the real rates of interest charged on bank loans are negative and partly because credit is still rationed. In any case, local governments do not like to see their banks remit excess reserves to the next level in the hierarchy, or to see their banks lend excess reserves to those in other localities – even to other branches of the same bank. Since local governments effectively control local banks, especially the careers of their managers, local banks have to heed local government priorities and to act in the 'interest of the locality' rather than in pursuit of pure profits. Thus, local extra-budgetary investments have often become a major source of credit expansion regardless of the national credit policy. Further, financial decentralisation has not led to financial autonomy. On the contrary, giving banks 'autonomy' actually means passing the control of financial resources to local governments.

Decentralization dilemmas have created a host of problems for the central government:

1. *Regional Protectionism*. With decentralisation, local governments have come to depend heavily on the financial health of local enterprises for their revenues, and local officials often have to intervene whenever possible to protect their resources and markets. This gave rise to the

widespread practice called 'local protectionism', which has resulted in the fragmentation of domestic product markets, the immobility of resources and uneconomic regional specialisation. Virtually all levels of local governments – from province to town – have in varying degrees imposed barriers that prevent or impede access to their local market.[31] In regions well endowed with raw materials, the local authorities have an incentive to establish their own regional processing industry, since this is more profitable than selling the raw materials to other regions. Hence, inter-regional sales of raw materials are restricted. Sometimes local authorities intervene to forcibly stop their local raw materials from flowing to other regions or to restrict the importation of production from factories outside their locality. Some even deployed local militia to set up check-points on the highways and to patrol county borders. The Chinese media in recent years have frequently reported the events of the 'Silkworm War', 'Wool War', 'Tea War', 'Tobacco War', 'Coal War', and 'Cotton War'.

2. *Allocative Inefficiency*. Local governments are motivated to pursue the objective of maximising revenue, which is not necessarily the same as profit maximisation. As a result, local investment decisions may not be based on efficiency considerations.[32]. In recent years, governments of many localities have concentrated investments on a few consumer goods such as household electrical appliances, beverages and cigarettes in blatant disregard for the economies of scale and cost advantages. These high-cost industries, often supported by cheap capital subsidised by local banks, operated on soft budget constraints. The result is the duplication of investments and the proliferation of many small-scale but high-cost industries, much like the inefficient 'import substitution industries' in many Third World countries. Consequently, many localities have built up a fragile industrial base with serious structural imbalance on account of excess investment in processing industries and under-investment in bottleneck sectors such as energy, transportation and basic infrastructure. This has created a big dilemma for the central government, which, constrained by its diminishing fiscal resources, found it difficult to fund the needed investments in infrastructure and basic industry.

3. *Macroeconomic Instability*. Administratiive decentralisation, in weakening the fiscal position of the central government, has also undermined its ability to carry out its macroeconomic stabilisation functions. Macroeconomic instability has become a serious systemic problem of the Chinese economy. Since 1979 the Chinese economy has gone through three distinct business cycles, which were partly caused by the half-reformed nature of the economy and partly due to the lack of built-in stabilisers. When the economy gets overheated, the central government could not employ the usual macroeconomic fine-tuning techniques of fiscal and monetary policies for stablisation.[33] On the other hand, local govenments, with their extra-budgetary fiscal resources, are often free to

pursue their ambitious expansion programmes with scant regard for the overall national macroeconomic conditions. This not only complicates the stabilisation task of central government but also aggravates the instablity of the national economy. As a matter of fact, most local officials oppose tight monetary and fiscal policies, because such policies would hinder the growth of their local budgetary revenues and affect their industrial development and employment creation. They would therefore openly or indirectly undermine or counteract the centre's macroeconomic policies. Hence the common phrase in China: 'The centre may issue its policy directives, the locality would always be able to cope with its own strategy.' When there is a clash of policy objectives between central and local governments, the latter would almost always have the upper hand, since it is the latter that controls tax collection and influences the local banks.

4. *Government Involvement in Business*. To overcome fiscal difficulties, the central government adopted many measures such as increasing its claims on budgetary resources or re-dividing its responsibilities with local governments. Local governments, however, have sought to protect their fiscal resources by 'defensive entrepreneurialism' and 'institutional creativity'.[34] One way is to tap enterprise funds by imposing a variety of informal levies.[35]

Another highly popular way is to start their own commercial operations by setting up the Chinese style government-links companies (GLCs). With privileges and power, GLCs are definitely in a strong position to reap profits through making use of opportunites generated by the market-oriented reform and collecting economic rents. Creation of GLCs also helps ease overstaffing in the government organisation and increases the income of underpaid civil servants. The result is a new spate of government involvement in business which has profound implications on the economic role of government.[36] In 1992, newly registered enterprises amounted to 1.25 million, and about ten per cent of them were set up by party and government organisations.

In a market economy, the primary rationale of government economic intervention is to correct market failures and to foster competition. In so doing, the government is supposed to play a neutral role as an umpire among different market participants. With its increasing involvement in business through the GLCs, the Chinese government (though mainly local goverments) itself becomes a big player in the market and loses its credibility as a neutral umpire. Furthermore, the current institutional environment actually encourages more rent-seeking activities or even open corruption, since there are virtually no clear rules and regulations to determine how the government should interface with business. Such increasing direct government involvement in business may institutionalise corruption and lead to the possible emergence of bureaucratic capitalism.[37]

Having discussed these dilemmas and problems, one should not under-estimate the important advantages of decentralisation. Perhaps the greatest advantage has been to create interest groups in favour of further reforms.[38] As discussed above, the decentralisation approach of reform has benefited local government officials by vastly expanding their power and economic authority. Therefore, local government officials would naturally identify themselves with the reformers at the centre and seek to preserve what they have gained in the decentralisation process. This was evident during the period following the Tianamen tragedy in 1989 when local governments counteracted the reversal of reforms by the conserva-tives at the centre, frustrated the attempts to close semi-private rural enterprises, blunted the exertions of recentralisation of financial revenues and material allocation, and kept reform initiatives alive.[39] Hence, de-centralisation has brought local government officials into the reformist camp, and changed the relative power of the anti-reform and pro-reform forces within China's decision-making system. In such a setting, local governments have gradually replaced the bureaucrats of the functional departments at the central level to become the major sources of political support to the reformist leadership at the centre. Deng Xiaoping's tour of South China in 1992 can be seen as an all-out effort to gather support from provincial leaders in order to break down the reform deadlock at the centre.

Decentralisation has also generated a reorientation of the interest of the bureaucracy away from rent-seeking toward economic performance, and fostered a climate for reform initatives and spontaneous reform at the local level. The central budgetary revenue has been significantly reduced as a result of decentralisation, which implies that the benefits that local governments could gain from bargaining and negotiating with the centre have also been drastically reduced. At the same time, the 'Revenue Sharing System' of 1980 has also in part defined the property rights for local governments and made them the residual claimants of their regions,[40] thus greatly increasing the benefits they could secure from extra-budgetary revenues and local economic growth. Therefore, decentralisation has redirected the interests of local governments to economic reform and system renovation. The continuation of such a process would, in the long run, change the bureaucrats' mentality towards market operations and bring them to the realisation of the new roles they have to play in the market environment.

Finally, decentralisation has the advantage of allowing a diversity of localities to accommodate to differences in preferences. Different policy innovations are implemented in different regions, and only successful ones would spread to other regions. Such a procedure could avoid policy failure in the scale of the whole nation. Furthermore, when one province moves ahead, its neighbours are compelled to follow. More prosperous regions would attract more resources such as foreign capital and human capital. Therefore, competition among localities provides additional incentives for local governments to change, to adapt to changes in consumer preferences and technology, and to innovate.[41] Reform has extended the competition into new fields such as enhancing the quality of consumer products produced by local industry in order to occupy bigger market shares, or improving of the investment environment in order to attract more foreign investors to the region. In fact, the problems of regional protectionism mentioned above can be used to understand the intensity of such competition. In general, and taken over the long run, the decentralisation process has helped to create pro-reform and pro-development local governments, which makes China's reform process self-reinforcing and irreversible.

V: AN UNCERTAIN ROLE

It is thus clear that the economic role of the Chinese government, both at the central and local levels, has undergone great changes in the reform era. Most prices have been decontrolled, enterprise controls relaxed, mandatory plans abolished, the role of the state as a producer shrunk, and the role of state as a financier diminished. These changes for the central government are drastic but on the whole positive, since it permits a bigger role for the market. While the role of government at the national level has diminished, the role of government at local level has vastly expanded. In China as in other transitional economies, economic reform and administrative decentralisation go hand in hand. As a result, the role and functions of local governments at all levels have also been greatly transformed in the reform process, with local governments becoming an integral part of China's self-reinforcing reform process. If the reduced role of the central government has been a positive factor for China's recent economic growth, the enhanced role of local governments has brought about serious dilemmas and problems. Major problems like protectionism, allocative inefficiency, macroeconomic instablity, and increasing government involvement in business have briefly been reviewed in this paper. The central government in Beijing is very much in a quandary about how to cope with these problems.

From the standpoint of the central government, therefore, decentralisation has probably created as many problems as it has resolved. In fact, some quarters in Beijing have come round to see the new danger of over-decentralisation. As an authoritarian one-party government ruling a huge unitary state of 1.2 billion population, Beijing appears on the surface very strong and powerful. In actual fact, Beijing is rather weak in terms of state capacity, as reflected by its limited command of national economic resources. The revenue–GNP ratio declined sharply from 31.2 per cent in

1978 to 14.7 per cent in 1992 – of which only 40 per cent was earmarked for the centre. Never before in modern Chinese history has the financial position of the central government been so weak.[42] Reform has whittled away the economic base of the centre.

Historically, a weakened centre in China was always a prelude to internal chaos caused by rising regionalism and war-lordism. This potential danger has apparently not been lost to the current leadership in Beijing. In November 1993, the Third Plenum of the 14th Central Committee of the Party adopted a 50-article 'Decision', which sets out new guidelines to deal with the many pressing problems created by reform. Among the new reform initatives, the most crucial are the packages for fiscal and monetary reforms, which are aimed at increasing the state capacity of the central government in terms of macroeconomic management. However, it is uncertain at this point if the new reform measures could effectively stem the decline of the centre, much depending on how far local governments will cooperate in carrying out these reforms.

The Chinese economy has been heading for the export-oriented development strategies which other East Asian economies have successfully executed. On the eve of the open-door policy in 1978, China's total foreign trade was only US$9.8 billion. By 1993, China's total trade turnover increased 20 times to US$196 billion, making China the world's 11th largest trading nation. An intriguing question can therefore be posed: is the economic role of the Chinese government going to evolve much in the same style of other East Asian governments, which is highly interventionist and yet 'growth effective', especially in terms of pushing for the dynamic expansion of their manufactured exports?[43] It seems likely that such a developmental role will be played out more effectively by various local governments than by the central government.

NOTES

1. P. Streeten, 'Against Minimalism', in L. Putterman and D. Rueschemeyer (eds), *State and Market in Development: Synergy or Rivalry?* (London, 1992).
2. The World Bank has argued that the best approach to economic development, as exemplified by the successful Asia-Pacific economies, is to adopt the 'market-friendly' strategy which is associated with effective but carefully delimited positive government interventionism in terms of getting the price right. See World Bank, *World Development Report 1991* (Washington DC, 1991).
3. K. Lieberthal and M. Oksenberg, *Policy Making in China: Leaders, Structures, and Processes* (Princeton, 1988).
4. R. Ericson, 'The Classical Soviet-Type Economy: Nature of the System and Implication for Reform', *Journal of Economic Perspectives*, Vol.5 (1991) pp.11–27.
5. R.A. Musgrave, *The Theory of Public Finance* (New York, 1959).
6. The government has a double role to play in its relations with enterprises. It not only has the authority to collect taxes from enterprises, but also has the right to claim residual profits as the owner. As long as prices are controlled by the government, it makes no difference if the revenue is formally collected as a turnover tax or as residual profit remitted to the state. See R.I. McKinnon, 'Macroeconomic Control in Liberalizing

Socialist Economies: Asian and European Parallels', in A. Giovannini (ed.), *Finance and Development Issues and Experience* (Cambridge, 1993).

7. P Murrell and M. Olsen, 'The Devolution of Centrally Planned Economies', *Journal of Comparative Economics*, Vol.15 (1991), pp.239–65.

8. McKinnon, 'Macroeconomic Control'.

9. Ericson, 'The Classical Soviet-Type Economy'.

10. Extra-budgetary revenue of local governments expanded to 31 per cent of total budgetary revenue in 1978 from only 7.8 per cent in 1952. Extra-budgetary revenue of the SOEs and their supervising agencies, amounting to 22.5 per cent of total budgetary revenue in 1978, has since become very important in financing extra-budgetary investment projects in the reform era.

11. J. Burkhead, 'The Changing Economic Role of Government', in Warren Samuels (ed.), *Fundamentals of the Economic Role of Government* (New York, 1989).

12. Ruan categorised the political forces within the Party into four groups by making a distinction between 'new authoritarian reformers' and 'old authoritarian reformers'. However, there is little difference between these two groups except that the 'new authoritarian reformers' are more tolerant and less high-handed toward the pro-democracy movement. See M. Ruan, 'On Objectives and Strategies of the Democracy Movement', in Jia Hao (ed.), *The Democracy Movement of 1989 and China's Future* (Chinese Edition, Washington DC, 1990).

13. Former party general secretary, Hu Yaobang, represented this group.

14. Den Xiaoping and Zhao Ziyang (a former premier and general secretary of the Party) are the major figures in this group.

15. This group has the strongest foundation within the Party because of its orthodox positions. Chen Yun, the former chairman of the Party's central advisory committee, is one of the most important figures in this group.

16. S. Su, 'The Impacts and Origins of the 1989 Democracy Movement', in Jia Hao (ed.), *The Democracy Movement of 1989 and China's Future* (Chinese Edition, Washington DC, 1990).

17. 'Preliminary Suggestions on the Economic System Reform' drafted by the State Council's Economic System Reform Office was the first significant attempt to adopt the market-oriented reform. See J. Wu, *Jihua Jingji Haishi Shichang Jingji (Planned Economy or Market Economy)* (Beijing, 1993), p.135.

18. Prior to reform, no assignment of expenditure responsibilities or revenue-raising capability was made between the central and local governments. The local budgets and that of the central government were treated as one. This policy of 'eating out of one big pot' led to acknowledged waste, inefficiency and reduced tax effort on the part of local governments. Reform intended to address this problem, and therefore the system of 'eating out of separate kitchens' was introduced.

19. K. Chen, G. Jefferson and I Singh, 'Lessons from China's Economic Reform', *Journal of Comparative Economics*, Vol.16 (1992), pp.201–25.

20. There is little difference between 'commodity economy' and 'market economy' according to Chinese economists, except that 'commodity economy' is the term used in Soviet political economy text books and more familiar to Chinese officials who were usually trained under the Soviet system. See Wu, *Planned Economy or Market Economy*, p.169.

21. K. Chen, 'China's Economic Reform and Social Unrest', in Jia Hao (ed.), *The Democracy Movement of 1989 and China's Future* (English Edition, Washington DC, 1990). See also K. Chen, 'Price Reform: Gradual and Radical Approaches', paper presented at the First Workshop on Economic Management and Transition Towards a Market Economy, National University of Singapore, Singapore, 27–31 Oct. 1992.

22. Wu Jinglian, a professor from the Chinese Academy of Social Sciences, is the leading figure of this group, and he has been dubbed 'Market Wu'. See J. Wu and X. Zhou, *Zhongguo Jingji Gaige de Zhengti Sheji (The Integrated Design of China's Economic Reform)* Beijing, 1990.

23. Li Yining, a professor from Beijing University, is the key proponent in this group, and he has been dubbed 'Stock Li'.

24. K. Chen, 'The Failure of Recentralization in China: Interplay among Enterprises, Local Governments, and the Centre', in Arye L. Hillman (ed.), *Markets and Politicians: Politicized Economic Choice* (Boston, 1991).

25. World Bank, *China: Reform and the Role of the Plan in the 1990s* (Washington DC,

1992), Ch.2.
26. J. Wong, 'China Facing the Challenges of High Economic Growth and Further Reforms', paper written for the Union Bank of Switzerland's Risk Takers' (Investors) Seminar, Phuket, Thailand, 17–23 Feb. 1994.
27. G. White, 'Basic-Level Local Government and Economic Reform in Urban China', in Gordon White (ed.), *The Chinese State in the Era of Economic Reform* (New York, 1991).
28. C.P.W. Wong, 'Between Plan and Market: The Role of the Local Sector in Post-Mao China', *Journal of Comparative Economics*, Vol.11 (1987), pp.385–98.
29. K. Chen, 'Decentralisation and Changing Central-Local Relations in Transitional Economies', paper presented at the Second Workshop on Economic Management and Transition Towards a Market Economy, National University of Singapore, Singapore, 11–23 Oct. 1993.
30. C.P.W. Wong, 'Central–Local Relations in an Era of Fiscal Decline: The Paradox of Fiscal Decentralization in Post-Mao China', *China Quarterly*, Vol.128 (1991), pp.691–715.
31. Chen, 'Failure of Recentralization in China'.
32. C. Findlay, and J. Shu, 'Interest Group Conflicts in a Reforming Economy', in Andrew Watson (ed.), *Economic Reform and Social Change in China* (London and New York, 1992).
33. J. Wong, 'China Facing Challenges'.
34. White, 'Basic-Level Local Government'.
35. C. Wong, 'Central–Local Relations'.
36. J. Wong, 'Power and Market in Mainland China: The Danger of Increasing Government Involvement in Business', *Issues & Studies*, Vol.30 (1994), pp.1–12.
37. J. Wong, 'Power and Market'.
38. World Bank, 'Chinese Economic Reform Experience', in Morris Bornstein (ed.), *Comparative Economic Systems: Models and Cases* (Boston, MA, 1994), p.546.
39. K. Chen, 'Failure of Recentralisation in China'.
40. Z. Shi, 'Reform for Decentralisation and Reform by Decentralisation', paper presented at the International Symposium on the Theoretical and Practical Issues of Transition Towards Market Economy in China, Haikou, Hainan, China, 1–3 July 1993.
41. J.E. Stiglitz, 'On the Economic Role of the State', in J.E. Stiglitz *et al.*, *The Economic Role of the State* (Cambridge, MA, 1989).
42. S. Wang and A. Hu, 'Strengthening the Leading Role of the Central Government in China's Transition Towards a Market Economy', report presented to the National Development Strategy Studies Group of the Chinese Academy of Sciences, (Beijing, 1993).
43. For further discussion of the various roles of the high-performance East Asian economies, see World Bank, *The East Asian Miracle: Economic Growth and Public Policy* (Washington DC, 1993).

The Private Sector as the Engine of Philippine Growth: Can Heaven Wait?

MANUEL F. MONTES

I: INTRODUCTION

In the light of the prevailing development teleology which associates poor economic performance with government failure, the Philippine paradox can be stated simply: the Philippines finds itself being grouped among those economies with the poorest development prospects in East Asia, even though it has, and has had for a long period, the most extensive private economy in the region. Countries with strongly statist economic systems in the region, such as China and Vietnam (not to mention the extreme backwardness of these countries relative to the Philippines in the matter of modern business practices and contractual and legal systems) have generated greater international interest than the Philippines as the region's 'next tigers'. An examination of the Philippine paradox has the potential of throwing critical light on prevailing approaches to development and economic reform. We shall first review the state of Philippine development (in Section II) and identify the bases for the country's relatively dimmer economic prospects. In Section III, we shall examine the role of the state in the economy and demonstrate the other part of the paradox – that comparatively the Philippine state does not participate in the economy as extensively as it does in other Asian countries. Nevertheless, the Philippine state has acquired a reputation as being in need of contracting its interventionist policies. In Section IV we explore the relationship between the state and the private sector as a first step in addressing the paradox. In Section V we propose a model to reconcile the disparate elements of the Philippine development experience.

II: STATIC ECONOMIC STRUCTURE

Between 1960 and 1991, the Philippine economy (GDP) has managed to grow at the rate of 3.96 per cent per year, or about two per cent per year in per capita (GNP) terms,[1] a record that would be the envy of the vast majority of developing countries. Based on macroeconomic statistics, the Philippine case is not a 'basket case', but instead one of a moderately successful economy, following a rather standard pattern of growth. Overall growth rates hovered around five per cent until 1983, implying that the country followed the pattern of most other countries in protecting its

Manuel F. Montes, East-West Center, Hawaii

growth rate from the oil price shocks by utilising foreign savings. Table 1 demonstrates, through the growth rates of investment by the non-financial public sector and non-financial public enterprises, that foreign savings mainly flowed through public investment.[2] In 1983–85, the combination[3] of the political legitimacy crisis of the martial law regime of Ferdinand Marcos and the country's accession to the world financial crisis saw the country's deepest economic collapse, registering as the negative 1.3 per cent rate of growth for GDP in 1980–85 (Table 1).

Through most of the post-war period, the Philippines followed the standard development pattern, in which industrial and manufacturing growth led other sectors. Manufacturing growth rate averaged 4.05 per cent through the whole period and peaked at 6.7 per cent per year in the early 1970s (Table 1); the average annual growth rate of agriculture was 3.06 per cent. What is startling about the Philippine experience is that in spite of the relatively steady growth over the 30-year period, the economy's structure changed very little. Over this period, agriculture's share of GDP fell from 30 per cent to 22 per cent, while that of manufacturing increased almost imperceptibly from 24.85 per cent to 25.45 per cent (Table 2). It is

TABLE 1

PHILIPPINE ECONOMIC GROWTH, 1960–91

(average annual growth rates, 1985 prices)

	1960-70	1970-75	1975-80	1980-85	1985-91	1960-91
GDP (market prices)	4.92	5.77	6.06	-1.27	3.62	3.96
Agriculture	4.28	3.00	5.03	-0.39	2.70	3.06
Industry	5.68	8.55	7.2	-4.09	5.01	4.33
Mining & quarrying	7.35	2.98	9.73	5.43	-1.39	4.91
Manufacturing	5.83	6.73	5.52	-3.09	4.82	4.05
Services	4.77	5.11	5.51	1.02	5.28	4.25
General Government Consumption	5.47	11.31	2.69	-2.81	5.78	4.21
Gross Domestic Investment	6.13	12.57	6.61	-11.45	13.15	4.50
Non-Financial Sector			24.40	-14.63	12.16	.
Non-Financial Public Enterprises			27.58	-14.82	7.91	
Private Sector			5.51	-5.43	8.71	
Imports	5.29	5.69	11.12	-6.95	16.54	5.61
Exports	4.78	4.37	15.23	-2.40	9.90	5.93
Gross Domestic Saving	6.51	0.00	12.37	-7.18	3.97	3.43

Source: National Census and Statistical Board, Statistical Yearbooks.

TABLE 2

PHILIPPINE ECONOMIC STRUCTURE, 1960–91

(as % of GDP)

	1960	1965	1970	1975	1980	1985	1990
GDP (market prices)	100.00	100.00	100.00	100.00	100.00	100.00	100.00
Agriculture	29.97	29.88	28.18	24.68	23.50	24.58	22.45
Industry	31.37	32.13	33.70	38.38	40.52	35.07	35.82
Mining & quarrying	1.15	1.00	1.44	1.26	1.50	2.08	1.55
Manufacturing	24.85	24.47	27.07	28.32	27.60	25.15	25.45
Services	38.66	37.98	38.12	36.94	35.98	40.35	41.73
General Government Consumption	7.11	7.00	7.49	9.67	8.23	7.61	8.06
Gross Domestic Investment	16.83	20.83	18.86	25.75	26.41	15.33	22.74
Non-Financial Sector				3.46	7.69	3.72	5.28
Non-Financial Public Enterprises				1.81	4.56	2.18	2.55
Private Sector				17.48	17.03	13.74	16.68
Imports	22.62	21.92	23.41	23.32	29.43	21.89	37.64
Exports	18.17	24.19	17.93	16.77	25.38	23.96	30.72
Resource Balance	-4.44	2.27	-5.4	-6.55	-4.06	2.07	-6.91
Gross Domestic Saving	21.84	17.02	25.38	19.17	25.59	18.80	18.27

Source: National Census and Statistical Board, Statistical Yearbooks.

as if, except for trend influences from such inexorable factors as the population growth rate which started at three per cent in the early 1960s and has fallen to 2.4 per cent, the economy has primarily grown all of its parts proportionately. It is also the case that, based on family income and expenditure surveys, the Gini measure of income inequality has hovered in the narrow range of 0.45 to 0.50.[4]

The comparison with Thailand's structural change is dramatic as shown in Figure 1 where we plot the proportion of GDP in manufacturing against that in agriculture for both Thailand and the Philippines for each year from 1960 to 1991. In 1960, the Phillipines leads Thailand by about ten years in structural terms, then proceeds to spend the next 30 years rotating around a narrow region, while Thailand steadily increases its manufacturing capability. Based on the National Census and Statistics Office data, industry absorbed 16.5 per cent of employed Filipinos in 1970; in 1990, this proportion had actually declined somewhat to 15.5 per cent. In the same period, the proportion employed in services increased from 29.7 per cent to 33 per cent. Agriculture accounted for 53.8 per cent of employment in 1970 and 51.5 per cent in 1990.

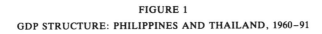

FIGURE 1

GDP STRUCTURE: PHILIPPINES AND THAILAND, 1960-91

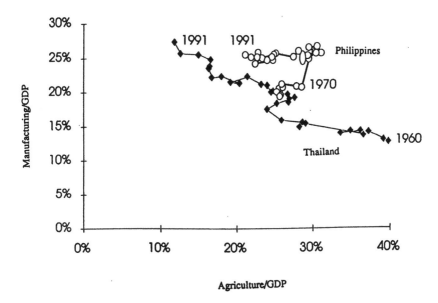

The prospects for the Philippine economy can be interpreted from the information in Tables 1 and 2. The country has experienced negative growth since the onset of the 1990s due to a variety of natural, infrastructural, structural, and policy factors. The structural and policy factors, and their interaction, concern us most here. Beyond the natural disasters, the most prominent being the eruption of volcano Mount Pinatubo located 50 kilometres north-east of Manila, infrastructural bottlenecks have been blamed for the negative growth rates in the early 1990s. Inadequate power supply, causing ten hour outages constrained production in 1990–93. With government attention, the power bottleneck is being solved, but its very onset exposes government capacities and response patterns. The power deficit emerged from government inattention and bureaucratic inability to elevate the priorty of the problem, in spite of intense interest and promotion from potential bilateral and multilateral donors. The initial policy response was to encourage the private sector[5] to install its own alternative capacity. The policy eased the problem temporarily,[6] created a profitable 'industry' in installing these sets both in businesses and the private homes of the wealthy, and represented investment that did not result in new manufacturing capacity and/or in an increase in labour absorption.

The private sector accounts for 68 to 73 per cent of total investment (not taking into account that inventory changes are also undertaken mostly by the private sector) based on the numbers of Table 2, which are already skewed against the private sector since the data begins from 1975 during the petrodollar recycling period.[7] As a structural matter, the recovery of private investment vitality is critical for future growth. Policy conflicts in almost all key areas provide the 'excuse' for private sector investment uncertainty. The uncompleted agrarian reform programme (and the unresolved social justice issues therein), the structural and liberalisation programmes[8] which have pitted agricultural against manufacturing interests and importers against exporters, and the public sector's debt overhang and its fragile finances are outstanding examples. Beyond the 'excuse' of uncertainty are deeper structural factors such as the nature of state and business relations and the nature of the Philippine private sector itself, which we shall explore in the final section of this paper. If it is the case that the private sector leans heavily on the state in resolving its domestic investment dilemmas and if, indeed, the Philippines succeeds in diminishing the state's role in identifying investment priorities in accordance with prevailing development theory and the government's own stated intentions, the prospects of faster growth, not to mention faster structural change, are not very bright.

III: THE STATE AND THE PRIVATE SECTOR IN THE PHILIPPINE ECONOMY

At the level of macroeconomic statistics, the participation of the Philippine government in the economy is the least in Southeast Asia and lower than the renowned East Asian economies in Japan, Korea, and Taiwan. Table 3 provides a comparative listing based on current government revenue as a proportion of GDP from 1970 to 1990. Singapore followed by Malaysia has the highest participation among the countries in the table. The size of government participation is made larger beyond its current revenue by its ability to borrow and the investment programmes of its public enterprises. Table 4 demonstrates that before its foreign debt crisis in 1983 Philippine central government expenditure as a proportion of GDP lagged behind that of other East Asian countries except for Taiwan. At the peak of Philippine external borrowing, ironically during the foreign-donor supported recovery programme under the Aquino government, government expenditure as a proportion of GDP peaked at 22.7 per cent in 1987 (not shown in the table). Based on the size of current account deficits in the 1970s, Indonesia's and Malaysia's rate of external borrowing were not perceptibly smaller than that of the Philippines.

In the matter of public enterprises, in 1985, the sales of the Philippines' so-called 14 major non-financial government corporations (the non-major companies being mostly moribund, not directly economic such as the Boy Scouts Corporation, or too small to matter) accounted for 9.8 per cent of GDP; this proportion had been reduced to 7.8 per cent in 1990 as a result of the privatisation programme. Contrast this with the role of public non-

TABLE 3
CENTRAL GOVERNMENT CURRENT REVENUES
(% of GDP)

	1970	1975	1980	1985	1990
NIEs					
Korea	15.38	15.15	17.96	17.22	18.58
Singapore	22.41	25.36	26.38	37.93	na
Taiwan	na	15.46	14.67	13.91	16.77
ASEAN - 4					
Indonesia	10.77	18.19	22.90	20.98	na
Malaysia	19.88	22.95	26.12	27.23	na
Philippines	11.44	14.52	14.01	12.00	16.61
Thailand	12.81	12.55	14.42	16.08	19.72

Source: IMF, International Financial Statistics.

TABLE 4
CENTRAL GOVERNMENT EXPENDITURES
(% of GDP)

	1970	1975	1980	1985	1990	1991
NIEs						
Korea	16.3	15.7	17.3	16.5	16.8	15.8
Singapore	19.9	18.0	20.0	27.2	na	na
Taiwan	na	11.4	12.0	12.5	14.3	14.1
ASEAN - 4						
Indonesia	13.8	20.5	23.8	21.4	na	na
Malaysia	22.4	27.6	35.6	30.8	na	na
Philippines	11.3	15.1	13.4	11.2	20.0	19.5
Thailand	16.5	14.6	18.9	21.4	15.0	na
SOUTH ASIA						
Bangladesh	9.4a	6.5	10.1	12.5	14.9b	na
Burma	16.0a	12.7	15.8	16.1	na	na
India	9.1	11.8	13.3	16.4	17.3	na
Nepal	7.8	10.1	14.3	18.5	20.1	na
Pakistan	16.6	17.6	17.5	19.8	23.2	22.3
Sri Lanka	26.3	25.3	41.4	33.4	28.3	26.9

Notes: (a) 1973; (b) 1989.
Sources: IMF, International Financial Statistics; Central Bank of China, Taiwan, Financial
Statistics.

financial corporations in other Southeast Asian economies. Malaysia carried out extensive nationalisation of enterprises after 1969, with a state policy aimed at redressing income inequality through government control of enterprises in all key areas of the economy, holding stock on behalf of the Malay population (the Bumiputera group) and providing financing for proposed projects from Bumiputera bureaucrats and businessmen. The Indonesian government established enterprises to contribute to national development, especially in the area of public utility provision, to complement and support private enterprises in related economic areas, and to make profits and contribute to government revenues.[9] Government participation is prominent in oil and natural gas, utilities, steel, aluminium, fertiliser, cement, sugar refining, transportation and communications. Based only on the enterprises officially recognised as being owned by the national government, the sales of public sector enterprises accounted for two-thirds of Indonesia's GDP in 1986–87.[10]

The Philippines qualified for privatisation-motivated financing from the Bretton Woods agencies in the 1980s not because it required assistance to retreat from a socialist-style or even Asian-style public enterprise sector. The 1973 Constitution, completed under the martial law regime of Ferdinand Marcos, identified the private sector as the engine of growth, and similar statements are found in the 1987 post-Marcos Constitution. The public sector had grown precisely through the publicly channelled and guaranteed recycling of petrodollars under the auspices of international donors in the 1970s and grew even more rapidly in the early 1980s when the government honoured its guarantees on the private projects that had failed by infusing equity into these companies.

Independence from the US in 1946 did not spark a programme of nationalisation of colonial enterprises, as in the neighbouring countries of Malaysia and Indonesia.[11] Under the terms of the grant of independence, the Philippines accorded national treatment to American enterprises, which, as a consequence, could not have been the object of nationalisation. Eventually many of these enterprises were 'Filipinised' when, under decidedly market conditions, key Filipino business groups bought out controlling American interests.

The extensive role played by state enterprises in Japan, Taiwan,[12] and Korea stands in sharp contrast to a record in which, save for electrical generation and the small national railways company, the private sector was predominant in the provision of public utilities. Since 1937, 50 years before it became so in Japan, telephone services have been privately run in the Philippines; foreign companies have supplied petroleum refining and distribution services (except after the oil crisis when a government corporation purchased control of two companies, again partly at that time because the government had an advantage in obtaining oil supplies through diplomacy). The 'national airline' company was controlled by private interests, until it was nationalised under the Marcos regime during the 1970s, driven into debt difficulties, and taken over by a government pension fund, and subsequently control was sold to private interests by the Aquino government in 1992.

Two other indicators illustrate the 'privateness' of the Philippine economy. In 1980, before Japan and Korea began their financial liberalisation, the Philippine banking sector traded such a rich variety of financial instruments that a study by the World Bank and the IMF conceded that the financial system was 'quite sophisticated for [the country's] level of development'.[13] Half of secondary and 85 per cent of tertiary education is not only privately provided but indeed privately financed. Based on standard Western indices which rely on the extent of the public economy as a measure of the private economy, the Philippine economy ranks among the most private, if not the most private, among the Asian economies.

IV: THE STATE AND THE PHILIPPINE PRIVATE SECTOR

In the Asian context many Western measures of public participation are unreliable. The most often cited case is Singapore, in which extensive and large public corporations are engaged in economic activities but managed more professionally and with much less public capriciousness than the more famous large US corporations. The key difference between Western and Asian conceptions is that society, represented by the state[14] (often conceptualised in Confucian terms) precedes the private sector; therefore, the private sector, as one part of society, serves society and the state. More than formal legal systems (many of which are in an undeveloped state in comparison with that in the Philippines), traditions and hierarchical relations actualise this concept. In the Asian context, extensive state intervention in, supervision of, and coordination with the private sector occurs not only openly and without the presumption of undue bias,[15] but also with a reduced risk that particularistic private interests (and genuine private interests are by nature particularistic) will capture state policy, since the state stands above the private sector (and all subgroups therein). The other Southeast Asian economies do not have strong Confucian traditions but appear to have maintained states with a similar position in society and with sufficient 'strength' (defined as the capacity to design and implement policies independent of particularistic and foreign interests).

The Philippine state and the private sector operate within a more Anglo-American tradition, embodied in law and practice, which is intellectually grounded on a horizontal conception of society; political and economic contest as the means for uncovering what is best for society is a key element of this approach. The content of the state is thought to be empty, save for the protection of individual interests, prior to the outcome of such contests. Such a state does not have to be 'weak' so long as society acquiesces in the coercive character of social decisions. In the Philippines, however, the existence of independent power bases for the country's elite families so vividly examined in McCoy's[16] volume permits these to exempt themselves from such social decisions when advantageous, and to bend the social decision in their favour when they can attain political dominance (often temporary) in society. The civil service system is patterned after that of the US, with no provision for a cadre corps of public servants; the bureaucracy is weakened further by the frequent changes of party in power and the shifts in party alignments.

Philippine development plans have tended to be cheerleading exercises instead of decisions about which potential priorities have to be sacrificed in the current plan period. This mode of planning permits private interests to justify almost any project as being consistent with the current development plan. In 1989, the Supreme Court was petitioned (and saw fit) to rule on whether a petrochemical plant project, supported by the World Bank's International Finance Corporation (IFC), should be located in one province as opposed to another: the controversy resulted in the withdrawal from the project of its Taiwanese partners. When conflict can be avoided, Philippine industrial policy prefers the approach of treating equally economic activities that are legally (but not necessarily economically) equal.

Beyond horizontal conceptions of society, however, the state–private sector relationship in the Philippines collides with Western views of the state as an extraneous economic actor and of state intervention as the principal restraint to development. Philippine industrial policy, state credit programmes, and import protection provide the basis for the proposition, based on neo-classical economic thought, that government failure is the main culprit behind Philippine development failure. This is one way to resolve the Philippine paradox: by claiming that in spite of the fact that the state's economic role has been relatively more mild than that seen in more successful countries in the region, these policies are intrinsically harmful to development prospects. A string of studies[17] from 1971 to 1988 advance and recycle the theme of Philippine underdevelopment being rooted in state-created inefficiency; the indispensability of what has subsequently been termed 'market-oriented' reforms form the refrain of these studies.

While the long stretch of this discourse should, by itself, raise suspicions either about the accuracy[18] of or the political feasibility of the analysis, the very inability of successive Philippine governments to implement fully its policy ramifications generates a cycle of reincarnation for the same discourse as different generations of Filipino economists, domestic policy makers, and staff members of international agencies come of age. The power of neo-classical analysis is that by providing a measure with which to evaluate a real economy against an ideal one, important policy deficiencies can be identified, irrespective of comparative country experience and as long as only imperfect implementation of the insinuated reforms take place in the country under analysis. On the one hand, the Panglossian quality of this framework makes an assessment of its analytical accuracy impractical, whether by cross-country comparison or by time series analysis; on the other hand – even, for the sake of argument, accepting its accuracy – addressing seriously the question of political feasibility opens up a Pandora's box of deeper structural questions (deeper than issues of the existence of state intervention) about the nature of Philippine underdevelopment.

This Philippine discourse has recently been overtaken by the newly completed 'Asian miracles' research[19] conducted at the World Bank, whose results can be interpreted as another way to resolve the Philippine paradox. Instead of a perfect economy, this approach proposes that state interventionist policies can work as long as the government is 'perfect' in the specific sense that the state's interventions are (1) 'market-friendly' (terminology used in the study itself, with particular emphasis on 'outward orientation'), (2) inequality-reducing (in particular, emphatic of human resource development), *and* (3) generally immune from particularistic interests (state autonomy, in the language of political science). It is thus a definition based on the nature of state intervention (and would be empty in the absence of state economic intervention), and does not concern itself with the nature of the state or the structure of society. Without such a 'perfect' government, the results of the research propose that interventionist policies will yield the same debilitating influences on development.

While this framework appears to 'excuse' the success of only that tier of countries following Japan into the industrial age in this century, it is not clear that the analysis advances the theoretical discussion very much. It resolves the Philippine paradox by recognising that the Philippine government is not 'perfect' enough, and accordingly permits a recovery of the refrain that the Philippine state should avoid engaging in economic intervention. This raises the question: given the past record of imperfect economic reform and given that a 'perfect' government would be one in which such reforms could take place, what must happen in order to install such a 'perfect' Philippine government? Once again, it leads to a Pandora's box of deeper structural questions. The 'Asian miracles' framework shares with the older purely neo-classical framework an analytical engine that depends almost entirely on an understanding of how governments affect (mostly injure) the economy. In spite of the fact that this analytical approach lays great store for the role of the private sector, it ironically relies on a undifferentiated model of private behaviour and has limited apparatus for analysing how the private sector affects the government and the economy.

Our rejection of the standard economic explanation of the Philippine paradox leaves us to explain the basis of reproduction for a social structure of a 'weak' state interacting with a dependent private sector. Three key elements constitute an alternative model.

The nature of the private sector and the application of rent earnings

'Rent-seeking' has become a well-used construct in economic policy circles. Within the neo-classical approach, it is an awkward concept as a source of policy proposals. In Krueger's[20] original formulation, the real costs of rent-seeking emanate mainly from competition for government-created privileges, so that if there were no competition but instead, say, an orderly queue for these privileges, no social costs would arise from 'rent-seeking', even though (1) the standard economic deadweight losses would still issue from the original government intervention and (2) one might have a normative objection to the income distribution impact of rent allocation. International policy advisers are well-advised to stay well clear of normative judgements of the latter, while the deadweight losses would subside automatically with the removal of the government pro-gramme, a case that would not be helped by assisting the design of an orderly queue.[21]

The Philippine experience suggests that focusing attention on the more classic definition of rents, that is those returns over and beyhond the economic opportunity earnings such as extra earnings obtained from enjoying a favourable location, provides a more flexible analytical tool; rent-seeking of the neo-classical type would be an extraneous concept. In the Philippines and the rest of Asia, private returns obtained beyond what might have been possible using, say, world prices would be rents. The critical difference between the Philippines and the more successful Asian economies is not that there were no rents, as we propose to define them, created out of state intervention operating through social processes of political positioning. With their more extensive state intervention, it is likely that the more successful Asian economies created more rents as a proportion of output. The difference lies in the nature of the state, the nature of the private sector and the uses to which rent-created resources were directed.

In the Confucian societies, irrespective of whether their private sectors were spawned from the state,[22] these rents are privileges granted by a higher authority, which has the right to monitor and supervise its use. The Confucian construct is not absolutely necessary to explain how rents might be utilised differently; all that is needed is differentiation between types of private sector institutions. First, there is the normal profit-seeking firm. Such a firm is able to advance its profits by reinvesting its surpluses in its own expansion and will tend to channel rents captured (and also profits earned) towards this purpose; such firms will continually seek to expand their scale, contribute to labour absorption, and in a competitive atmosphere are driven to innovate in order to lower costs. A different type of firm might 'trade on' its rent earnings, capturing rents through political influence and then applying those rents to retain or expand its protection and standing; such a firm finds its survival and expansion as more contingent on non-economic factors, even while paying its inputs their marginal costs. At start-up, many firms in different kinds of economies are of this 'rent-driven' type. If an economy is made up of a few large firms, one would expect most of them to be rent-driven. The expansion of these firms is more accidental on external factors and can be volatile, subject to swift changes in political fortune.

The firms which dominate Philippine society are of the latter type, at the same time that the state remains too 'weak' either to bend their invest-ments to conform with the social interest or intervene to provide an opening for other types of firms. These dominant firms are controlled by large family business groupings that have historically arisen out of land-holdings, rural credit, state allocations of war reparations finance after World War II, timber logging concessions, and perhaps the original land grants obtained during the Spanish colonial period (though the last is unlikely since in the time scale of decades the membership of this select group has been quite unstable). To secure development investment from these dominant groups, the state must offer a return-to-effort ratio that is competitive with that from land rents (both urban and agricultural), natural resource extraction, trading, and other traditional business activi-ties. Generalised liberalisation reforms, undertaken under the auspices of international assistance, dismantle the state's power to extend these benefits and weaken the state further, especially in terms of having the capacity to open channels for other types of firms to prosper. In any case, democratic political processes tend to ordain that the order of liberali-sation removes protection from those activities which have the greatest possibility for growth first and postpone those in slow growing industries,[23] undermining both the economic basis and the political constituency of these reforms over the medium term.

Competition with profound economic consequences among the elite in the sphere of politics

The second ingredient that sustains the Philippine political economy is political competition which has economic consequences for participants. In 1961, the economist Golay described the Philippine private sector thus: 'Filipino entrepreneurship is distinctly Filipino in its strong predilection to seek economic advantage through political institutions and processes.'[24] The rise of enterprises connected with the Marcos family and its friends during martial law, its political overthrow, and subsequent sequestration and 'privatisation' back to previous owners of consequential economic assets provides the best example. McCoy's volume[25] chronicles the intense political struggles among selected provincial families and the importance of their retaining political value to national leaders for the expansion and protection of their enterprises. Family groupings must invest a prudent part of their rental surpluses, if not also their profits, in these political struggles to maintain their economic standing in society; this is the role of political competition to the workings of the model. The economic role of this ingredient is that it situates the sphere of competition in the political arena, and devalues the importance of competition in the economic sphere. While political outcomes do play some role in conditioning economic outcomes in other societies, the relative weakness of the Philippine state as representor of the national collective interest in a healthy private-sector-as-a-whole amplifies this effect, so that an entrepreneur who seeks not to enter the politically determined arena must strive not to expand the scope of his business beyond that point at which he will begin encroaching on the business interests, including those only latent, of other important family groupings.

Expansion of the economic area, instead of structural change

The implication of the competition ingredient is that so long as the state is unable to represent more than the competing particularistic interests, distribution of flows of rental surpluses will correspond to changes in political outcomes. This politico-economic configuration offers limited support for private sector-led structural change. At its starkest, most abstract version, the economy would have little basis for growth, which conflicts with the fact that growth has occurred in the last 30 years. In fact, there is also the question of the source of rental surpluses, since these are, by definition, not generated within the production process. Natural resource based rents, derived either through (1) the difference between international prices and low domestic extraction costs and/or (2) government-controlled access to the resource are natural enough (pun intended). More complicated are rents from industrial promotion, since unlike the neo-classical Krueger approach, rental flows play a role in the model beyond their efficiency and income distribution effects. The ultimate source of rental resources from industrialisation policy come from (1) the state's tax revenues and (2) external financing.

The last is particularly important in providing the basis for the role of the state since in developing countries it has been the funnel through which international financing has ebbed and flowed in the past. In the

Philippine experience, the basing of US military facilities in this Cold War outpost whose society did not participate enthusiastically in the East–West struggle was an important influence in providing ready external finance for any sitting government. While the Philippines might be a private heaven, it is also a privateer's haven, with the state serving as the source of newly available rent resources packaged from foreign savings. With the withdrawal of the US bases and the government's poor tax performance, the Philippine state now operates with strongly diminished resources of this type.

The basis for growth in such an economy is the expansion of the economic area either through the opening of new natural resource extraction (especially goods that are exportable) or through the capture of new sources of international finance. Growth becomes heavily contingent on external events. Because of the conflicts spawned by internal expansion of economic activities, growth will tend to be proportional, as we noted in section 2, with the economy growing its subcomponents at the same rate. Because they are not classic capitalist economies, other Asian societies partake of different configurations of this framework. When private activities were creatures of the state in Japan and Korea, the state played a decisive hand in determining the flows of rent-generated resources. The relationship changes as relative private and state capabilities change. For example, Korean *chaebols*, even though creatures of the state, now challenge the state's economic leadership and without more genuine democratisation the society has the potential of reproducing a Philippine-type political economy, in view of the significant role the state had played in previous technological innovation, export-promotion and structural change. As might be for Korea, Philippine prospects for identifying a different growth pattern hinge on the emergence of new private actors or the retooling of existing private actors (with the accompanying reconfiguration of the state) whose dynamics rest more firmly on structural change and economic innovation.

NOTES

1. See James Boyce, *The Philippines: The Political Economy of Growth and Impoverishment in the Marcos Era* (Macmillan, 1993) pp.14–15.
2. As was the case for many developing countries as a result of the effort in the 1970s, successful on its own terms, by the Bretton Woods institutions to recycle rapidly the accumulating stock of petro-dollars.
3. The combination of these two factors is significant in a comparison with Indonesia which experienced a more extended period of shocks in the 1980s beginning with the collapse of oil prices, to the world debt crisis, and the subsequent revaluation of the Japanese yen in which most of Indonesia's foreign debt was denominated.
4. This is discussed in Manuel F. Montes, 'Philippine Income Distribution and Development', *Singapore Economic Review*, Vol.35, No.1 (October, 1993), pp.124–42. Table 2.10 in Boyce, *The Philippines*, p.24, reports the same pattern, though in the latter part of the chapter Boyce carries out extensive data adjustments to account for inadequate

coverage at the upper and lower ranges of the incomes to demonstrate the extent to which income distribution might have actually worsened.

5. Initially, the government removed the ban on imports of power sets and later permitted tariff free imports. This programme, while successful in its own terms, has subsequently been mired in controversy when the public learned that the Aquino government's president of the power corporation owned an interest in the most prominent power set importing company.

6. Temporarily, because these plants cannot substitute for base load capacity where the deficit actually resides.

7. The existence of the information from this period is explained by the availability of foreign technical assistance for data reconstruction within the post-debt crisis lending programme from the multilateral agencies.

8. For an example based on the tariff liberalisation episode of 1989 see Manuel F. Montes, 'The Politics of Liberalization: The Aquino Government's 1990 Tariff Reform Initiative', in David G. Timberman (ed.), *The Politics of Economic Reform in Southeast Asia* (Makati, Philippines, 1992), pp.91–115.

9. Amar Bhattacharya, Amar and Mari Pangestu, 'Indonesia: Development Transformation since 1965 and the Role of Public Policy', paper prepared for the World Bank Workshop on the Role of Government and East Asian Success, East-West Center, 19–21 Nov. 1992.

10. Naya, Seiji and William E. James, *Private Sector Development: A New Engine for Growth in Asian Developing Countries* (Resource Systems Institute, East-West Center, 2 Nov. 1989).

11. See Ismael Salleh, Yeah Kim Leng, and Saha Meyanathan, 'Growth, Equity, and Structural Transformation in Malaysia: Role of the Public Sector', paper prepared for the World Bank Workshop on the Role of Government and East Asian Success, East-West Center, 19–21 Nov. 1992.

12. For example in the 1950s state-owned enterprises accounted for an average 50 per cent of manufacturing value-added in Taiwan (see Yungchul Park, 'Development Lessons from Asia: The Role of Government in South Korea and Taiwan', *American Economic Review*, Vol.80 (1990), pp.118–21). See also Chalmers Johnson, 'Political Institutions and Economic Performance: The Government-Business Relationship in Japan, South Korea, and Taiwan', in F. Deyo (ed.), *The Political Economy of the New Asian Industrialism* (Cornell, 1987) and Robert Wade, 'The Role of Government in Overcoming Market Failure: Taiwan, Republic of Korea, and Japan', in H. Hughes (ed.), *Achieving Industrialization in East Asia* (Cambridge, 1988), pp.211–36.

13. The World Bank and the IMF, *The Philippines: Aspects of the Financial Sector: A Joint World Bank/IMF Study, East Asia and Pacific Regional Office* (The World Bank, Washington, DC, 1980), p.ii.

14. Manuel F. Montes and Keun Lee, 'An Interpretation of East and Southeast Asian Development in Light of Current Development Issues in China', East-West Center, paper presented at International Conference on East Asian Development: Lessons on Trade Policy and Regional Development, held in Guangzhou, China, 8–11 Nov. 1993, sponsored by the Development Research Centre of China and the East-West Center.

15. Confucian societies also stress merit-based ascent in the social hierarchy and consequently abhor the purchase of public office, even if indirectly through campaign contributions for Western-style electoral contests.

16. Alfred W. McCoy (ed.), *An Anarchy of Families: State and Family in the Philippines* (Madison, Wisconsin, 1993).

17. These studies are all listed in footnote 1, page 215 in Stephan Haggard, 'The Political Economy of the Philippine Debt Crisis', in Joan Nelson (ed.), *Economic Crisis and Policy Choice: The Politics of Adjustment in the Third World* (Princeton, 1990), pp.215–55.

18. 'Accuracy' meaning 'Is extensive structural transformation in the Philippines possible principally through the removal of state restraints on private sector behavior'.

19. World Bank, *The East Asian Miracle: Economic Growth and Public Policy*, World Bank Policy Research Reports (Oxford, 1993).

20. Anne O. Krueger, 'The Political Economy of the Rent-Seeking Society', *American Economic Review* (1974). Subsequent attempts to refine the concept (including the introduction of the phrase 'directly unproductive profit-seeking' (DUPS) activities) and to enlarge on its effects on society have been bounded by the unwillingness of its

proponenents to embark beyond the atomistic economic agents starting point of neo-classical economics.
21. Even though it is true that the losses from rent-seeking are less in Japan than in India, the Philippines, or Korea.
22. More true in Japan than in Korea and the Chinese economies.
23. See Joseph Y. Lim, Manuel F. Montes and Agnes R. Quisumbing, 'The Philippines', in Lance Taylor (ed.), *The Rocky Road to Reform* (Cambridge, Mass., 1993), pp.259–60 and Manuel F. Montes, 'The Politics of Liberalization: The Aquino Government's 1990 Tariff Reform Initiative', in ibid., p.98.
24. Frank H. Golay, *The Philippines: Public Policy and National Economic Development* (Ithaca, 1961), p.409.
25. McCoy, *Anarchy of Families*.